SoJourn

Volume 2, Number 1

A journal devoted to the history, culture, and geography of South Jersey

SJCHC

South Jersey Culture & History Center

Summer 2017

SoJourn is a collaborative effort. Local historians contribute the articles; Stockton students—in this issue, the editing interns of spring 2017—edit the articles, set the type and design the layout; the directors of the South Jersey Culture & History Center at Stockton University oversee the publication.

Editors
Elizabeth Birch, Taylor Cills, Kristen DeLeonard, Caroline Fanning, Anthony Ficcaglia, Sarah Galzerano, Angela Mazzara, Theresa McMackin, Diondra Meningall-Burney, Rebecca Muller, Alexa Novo, Olivia Oravets, Christina Pompper, Shilo Previti, Morgan Sacken, Michele Snyder, Victor Vorrath, Isola Webbe.

Editors in chief
Tom Kinsella and Paul W. Schopp

ISSN: 2474-6665

ISBN-13: 978-0-9976699-8-5

A publication of the South Jersey Culture & History Center
at Stockton University
www.stockton.edu/sjchc/

Filler images, at the conclusion of articles, courtesy of the Paul W. Schopp Collection unless otherwise noted.

To contact SJCHC write:
SJCHC / School of Arts & Humanities
Stockton University
101 Vera King Farris Drive
Galloway, New Jersey
08205

Email:
Thomas.Kinsella@stockton.edu
Paul.Schopp@stockton.edu

About this Issue of *SoJourn*

With the inaugural issue of *SoJourn*, we laid the keel, built the hull, and launched the boat. We began our cruise with *SoJourn* 1.2. Now, as we enter our second year, we continue sailing through the smooth seas and sometimes choppy waters of history and culture in South Jersey. Along our way, we have introduced readers to myriad interesting topics, ranging from Nash's Cabin and Picker Tickets to historic cultural issues, icons, and constructs, but always with an eye toward educating and entertaining. We hope you find the reading selections in *SoJourn* 2.1 to be in the very best tradition of the previous issues. If you continue to be disappointed in not finding an article that addresses your particular passion, feel free to contact us or, even better, write an article yourself! You might think, "I'm not a writer," but our student intern editors and our staff editors can ably assist you to publish a discourse on your favorite topic that will contribute to the historical record and that you can show others with pride. We are always looking for more content for future issues of *SoJourn* and we know most of our readers have stories and history to share with others.

Paul W. Schopp
Assistant Director
South Jersey Culture & History Center
Stockton University

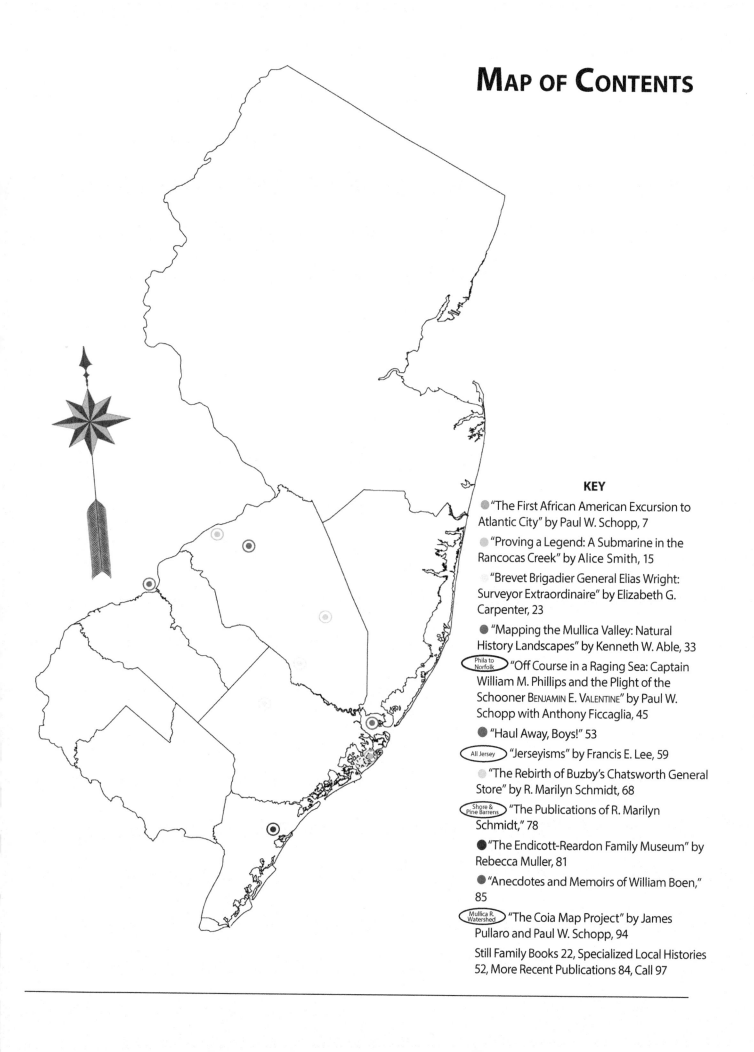

MAP OF CONTENTS

KEY

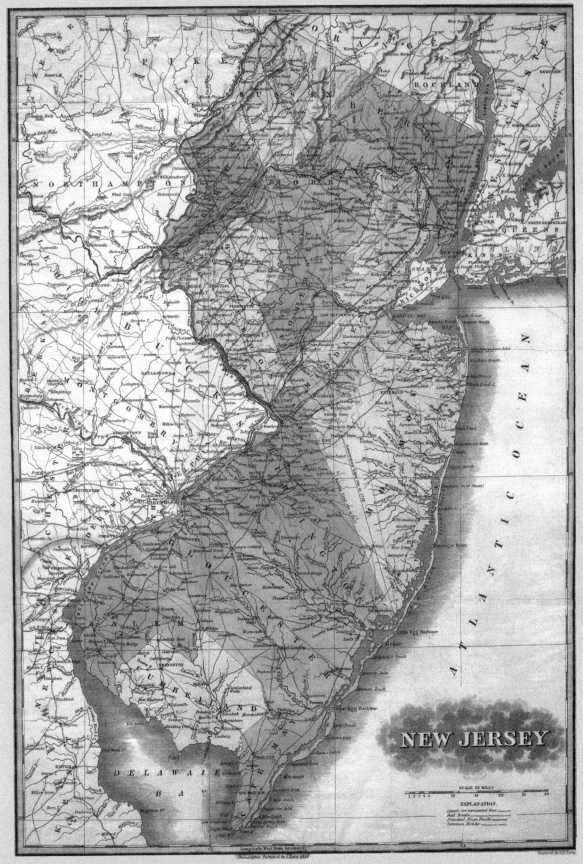

As Thomas F. Gordon prepared to publish his 1834 compilation, *A Gazetteer of the State of New Jersey*, he engaged Philadelphia map publisher Anthony Finley to create and print a map of New Jersey for inclusion with his book. Finley, in turn, contracted with James H. Young, an engraver residing at 3rd and Gaskill in the same city, to produce the finished copper plate for the intaglio printing of the map. With the plate in hand, Finley proceeded with the printing. When the ink dried, Finley hired colorists to hand tint the counties, the map's border frame, and the circular boundary line between Delaware and Pennsylvania. Either Finley or Gordon then folded each map so it could be bound into the finished gazetteer. Although small in size, this map is a place-name maven's dream, with toponyms ranging from Cabbagetown, Pickletown, Stockingtown and Poverty Beach to even calling out Campbell's Tavern in western Atlantic County. The map also shows the railroads then operating in New Jersey and the immediate surrounding areas, along with main roads. The Thomas F. Gordon that produced the gazetteer just described should not be confused with the Thomas Gordon that published the 1828 map of New Jersey. *Courtesy of the Paul W. Schopp Collection.*

The First African American Excursion to Atlantic City

Paul W. Schopp

As the first Camden and Atlantic Railroad train steamed into the new Atlantic City terminal in July 1854, a new era in transportation opened for those seeking to while away their summer days at a seaside resort. The attractive and healthy oceanside setting led many churches, fraternal organizations, and even businesses in the region to offer their constituents an opportunity to embark on day trips to Atlantic City called "excursions." Finding the experience appealing, excursions expanded in popularity as sponsors collaborated with the Camden and Atlantic management to secure a special, usually nonstop, express train carrying only passengers associated with the sponsoring organization. One such example, typical of an Atlantic City excursion, arrived on August 7, 1854, when Philadelphia-based employer Cornelius, Baker & Company sponsored an "Artizans' Excursion," detailed in the *Daily Pennsylvanian* the following day (Figure 1 below).

The excursion business proved quite lucrative to the Camden and Atlantic Railroad and the company sought to encourage an ever-increasing volume of such service. The corporate officers, superintendent, and/or the company's general agent left nothing to chance in ensuring excursionists experienced a thoroughly enjoyable outing. A review of various Philadelphia and New Jersey newspapers published during the second half of the nineteenth century confirms the scores of excursions offered to those of European ancestry living in the Quaker City and the Garden State. Some trips escaped the attention of the press or did not warrant public advertisement due to an available ready ridership.

During the initial eleven years of train service, white excursion sponsors systematically and categorically excluded African Americans from attending the special trip, leaving those facing racial animus to either arrive as singles or in small familial groupings by regular train service. Within months of the Civil War's cessation, however, documentary evidence illustrates that excursions began to be offered, albeit slowly, to people of color living in the greater Philadelphia area. While these black excursionists arrived in Atlantic City for just a day, the nascent resort contained a small, but important, population of permanent or semi-permanent African Americans. This group of black citizens became the backbone of the burgeoning city's expansive service industry at hotels, boarding houses, restaurants, and other related services. After contextualizing Atlantic City in the post-Civil War era with a brief discussion of those black residents who chose to work and live in the seaside town, and the segregated neighborhood that came to define them, this article will conclude with documentation of the first known excursion for people of color, sponsored by people of color.

AFRICAN AMERICANS IN THE NEWLY CREATED ATLANTIC CITY

When the Camden and Atlantic Railroad operated its first official train between its two termini on July 4, 1854, it established the seaside community of Atlantic City as one of the most enduring destinations for tourists throughout the Mid-Atlantic States and beyond. People of color initially arrived on Absecum Island to work in the hotels that lined the beachfront and provide labor for

The Artizans' Excursion.
☞ATLANTIC CITY, Aug. 7.—The Artizan Excursion train of Cornelius, Baker & Co.'s factories, which left Cooper's Point at 7 A. M. by the Camden and Atlantic Railroad, for Atlantic City, after passing the large glass manufacturing towns of Jackson, Waterford, Atsion and Winslow, all arrived here safely at 10½ o'clock. They had a truly delightful ride, the pleasure of which was much enhanced by many kind attentions received from Mr. Stone, the Chief Superintendent of the road. We are now in the full enjoyment of the various pleasures offered at the finest bathing grounds we have ever visited, the shooting and fishing being far superior to any place on the coast.

Figure 1. Artizans' Excursion, August 8, 1854.[1]

Table 1. 1860 Federal Decennial Census, Egg Harbor Township, Atlantic City Post Office[2]								
Name	Age	Sex	Race	Occupation	Real Estate	Personal Estate	Birth Place	Notes
Population Schedules, Page 1								
Thomas Almond	41	M	M	Barber			Va.	Worked and lived in hotel
William Jeffris (Head)	51	M	B	Shoemaker		$150	Pa.	
Beulah Jeffris	37	F	B				N.J.	
Theodore Brient	19	M	B	Laborer			N.J.	
Marshel Brient	8	M	B				N.J.	
Margaretta Brient	10	F	B				N.J.	All reside in same household
Dianna Measure	85	F	B				N.J.	
Mary Henryk	24	F	B	Servant			Del.	
Mary Morris	56	F	B				Va.	
Anthony Havre	56	M	B	Shoemaker			Pa.	
Population Schedules, Page 2								
Charles H. Green	17	M	M	Laborer			Del.	Worked and lived in hotel
Population Schedules, Page 5								
William Bright	52	M	B	Laborer			Pa.	
Mary Bright	49	M	B				Pa.	
Daniel Bright	13	M	B				N.J.	All reside in same household
Daniel Thompson	75	M	B	Gunning			Del.	
Population Schedules, Page 12								
Francenia Taylor	43	F	B	Servant			Pa.	Worked and lived in hotel
Population Schedules, Page 13								
Edward Garret	18	M	B	Servant			Del.	Worked and lived in hotel
Eliza Hopkins	25	F	B	Servant			Del.	Worked and lived in hotel
Anna Garret	45	F	B	Servant			Del.	Worked and lived in hotel
Hannah Garret	24	F	B	Servant			Del.	Worked and lived in hotel

other needs in the city. The 1860 federal decennial census (Table 1) reveals a total of twenty African Americans residing within the city limits.

It is currently unknown whether any of these people of color were fugitive slaves. It is possible that those who reported their birthplace as "New Jersey" could be runaways, but no evidence has been found to confirm this thesis. The 1870 federal decennial census failed to enumerate any of these individuals residing in Atlantic County, New Jersey. The census search included looking under both black and mulatto. Nonetheless, the 20 laborer- and artisan-class African Americans defined in the 1860 census served as the *de facto* foundation for a population of black citizens in Atlantic City. By 1900, this foundation swelled to become virtually 25 percent of Absecon Island's overall permanent citizenry, many of whom worked in the resort's service industries. Wielding considerable political power as a monolithic Republican voting block near the start of the twentieth century, they resided primarily in a city neighborhood known as Northside, grossly bounded as follows: on the east by Atlantic Avenue; on the north by Connecticut Avenue; on the west by Absecon Boulevard; and on the south by Arkansas Avenue. Figure 3 on the next page provides a more accurate delineation of the boundaries for the Northside neighborhood.

THE ROOTS OF BLACK TOURISM IN ATLANTIC CITY

Since tourists represent a transient population, the 1860 federal decennial census failed to enumerate any African Americans visiting the resort at that time, if indeed any had arrived before or during the census canvasser's circuit through Atlantic City. To date, no documentary evidence has come to light showing the presence of black tourism visitors in the city prior to 1862. In August of that year, however, a squib appeared in *The Christian Recorder*, house organ of the African Methodist Episcopal Church, stating,

> Mrs. S. Wailes has opened the Union Cottage for the accommodation of all who may desire to go to Atlantic City and spend a few days in recreation. We are informed that she has made quite extensive preparations. She will be pleased to have the pleasure of waiting on all who will favor her with their presence.[3]

Figure 3. Atlantic City's Northside[4, 5]

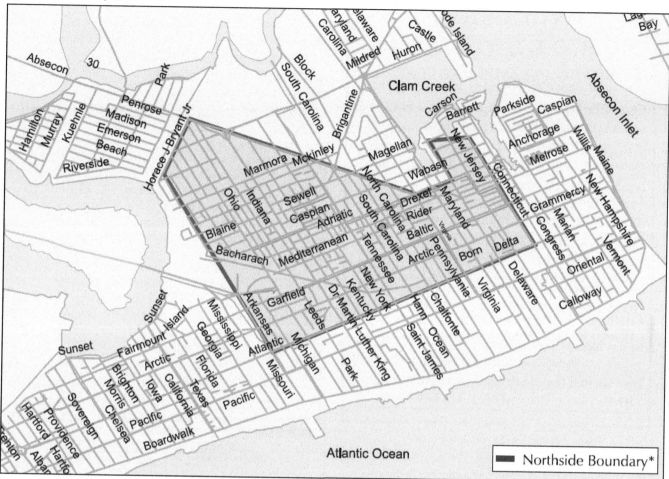

* The Northside boundary is based on the description of the Northside circa 1905 in Bryant Simon's *Boardwalk of Dreams*, p. 66.

The same issue carried an advertisement from Mrs. Wailes about her accommodations in Figure 4.

Mrs. Wailes likely selected the name "Union Cottage" to pay homage to President Abraham Lincoln's government and military at the time of the War of the Rebellion. The fact that Mrs. Wailes placed her advertise-

---

ADVERTISEMENTS.

"UNION COTTAGE."

ATLANTIC CITY, NEAR THE INLET.

The subscriber will always be happy to welcome her numerous friends, and the public in general.

PLANS :

Board per week,	. . . .	.	$4.00
" " day,	. . . .	.	1.25
Single meals,	. . . .	.	.50

S.H. WAILES, *Proprietress.*

Figure 4. Union Cottage advertisement, August 2, 1862.[6]

---

ment in a black newspaper during August 1862, hoping to attract those African Americans traveling to the resort after the season had officially ended for whites in Atlantic City, demonstrates that black tourism in the resort had begun. No further advertisements or notices appeared for the Union Cottage, so it is unclear how long Mrs. Wailes operated this boarding house, but this most likely represents the first offering of overnight accommodations specifically for black tourists in Atlantic City.

No notice of excursions exclusively for people of color can be found prior to 1865, although an advertisement for a special trip to the shore appearing two years earlier suggests that some African Americans might have taken advantage of previous excursions. John P. Harker, a merchant in Long-A-Coming, Waterford Township, Camden County (present-day Berlin), placed an advertisement that appeared in the June 27, 1863, edition of the *Camden Democrat* (Figure 5).

The fact that the excursion announcement included a conspicuous *Nota Bene* line of, "No Tickets sold to Colored Persons," suggests that some African Americans had managed to acquire tickets previously,

EXCURSION

FOR OLD OCEAN!

A GRAND PLEASURE EXCURSION FROM COOPER'S POINT TO ATLANTIC CITY,

On Friday, July 24, 1863

LEAVING VINE STREET WHARF AT SIX A. M.

Cooper's Point,	at	6.30	Junction	at	7.28
Haddonfield	"	6.50	Waterford	"	7.40
Ashland	"	6.58	Winslow	"	7.50
White Horse	"	7.07	Hammonton	"	7.58
Long-a-Coming	"	7.20	Weymouth	"	8.20

ARRIVING AT ATLANTIC CITY AT 9.25 A. M.

RETURNING; LEAVES ATLANTIC CITY at 5.30 P. M

Fare for the Round Trip, from Vine St. Wharf and Cooper's Point, $1 25.

From Haddonfield, Ashland, White Horse, Long-a-Coming, Junction, Waterford, Winslow, Hammonton, $1 00

TICKETS can be had at Vine Street Wharf, and of the Agents, at the above named Stations.

In order to secure Seats, purchase your Tickets early for this Pleasant Excursion.

No Tickets sold to Colored Persons.

The Subscriber respectfully solicits your patronage,

jy4 3t John P. Harker.

Figure 5. Harker's excursion, July 24, 1863.[7]

or the statement served simply as a preemptive measure. If given the opportunity for participating in such a trip, however, any African American ticketholders would have received directions from the train's conductor to sit in one of the two second-class coaches the company owned coupled to the rear of the train.[8] Segregated to inferior accommodations, far removed from the whites riding in first-class coaches, these black excursionists would have endured a lonely and degrading trip before enjoying their revelry on the beach. John P. Harker, the individual sponsoring the excursion, notably served in a variety of elected and appointed state and county political offices, first as a Whig and then as a Republican.[9,10] Consequently, discriminating against African Americans and excluding them from the excursion seems antithetical to his political philosophy as a mid-nineteenth-century Republican.

The First Excursion to Atlantic City for People of Color

The earliest railroad excursion operated between Philadelphia and Atlantic City by and for people of color that could be positively identified occurred on Tuesday, September 5, 1865—a mere five months after Confederate General Robert E. Lee surrendered to Union General Ulysses S. Grant, ending the Civil War. Perhaps the organizers and the attendees sought to test the extent of their freedoms at the end of a conflict fought to grant them such freedoms. A mention and advertisement for the first excursion appeared in the September 2, 1865, edition of *The Christian Recorder*:

> THE EXCURSION TO ATLANTIC CITY.
>
> In another column will be found an advertisement of an excursion from our friends to Atlantic City. It promises to be one of the most *recherché* of the season. The price of tickets is $1.25, which answers going and returning. From the names of those having the matter in charge, we anticipate it will be a success.
>
> Mr. Bryant, the well-known manager of the road [Camden and Atlantic], will spare no pains to provide for the comfort of all who may desire to attend. As this will probably be the last opportunity this season, we hope our friends will avail themselves of the same.[11]

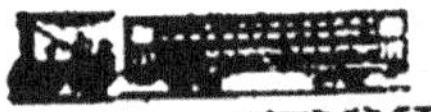

CAMDEN AND ATLANTIC RAILROAD.

SUMMER ARRANGEMENT.

THROUGH IN TWO HOURS.

On and after SATURDAY, July 1st, 1865, FIVE trains daily to Atlantic City, and one on Sunday.

TRAINS LEAVE VINE STREET FERRY

As follows:

Special Excursion..........6.30 A. M.
Mail Train..........7.30 A. M.
Freight, with Passenger Car attached...9.15 A. M.
Express, (through in Two Hours)..........2.00 P. M.
Atlantic Accommodation..........4.15 P. M.

RETURNING, LEAVE ATLANTIC:

Atlantic Accommodation..........5.47 A. M.
Express, (through in Two Hours)..........7.08 A. M.
Freight, with Passenger Car attached..11.47 A. M.
Mail Train..........4.45 P. M.
Special Excursion..........5.18 P. M.

SUNDAY MAIL TRAIN.

Leaves Vine Street Ferry at..........7.30 A. M
Returning, leaves Atlantic at..........4.45 P. M.

Fare to Atlantic $2. Round Trip Tickets, good only for the day and train on which they are issued, $3.

JUNCTION ACCOMMODATION.

Leaves Vine Street Ferry at..........5.30 P. M.
Leaves Jackson at..........6.28 A. M.

EXTRA HADDONFIELD TRAINS.

Leave Vine Street Ferry at 10.15 A. M. and 1.15 P. M.
Leave Haddonfield at 11.45 A. M. and 2.45 P. M.

N. B.—Freight must be delivered at Cooper's Point before 6 o'clock P. M., to insure its going down the next day.

je28-tf JOHN G. BRYANT, Agent.

Figure 6. Camden and Atlantic Railroad schedule, July 1865.[12]

The well-known and genial Camden and Atlantic general ticket agent, John G. Bryant, maintained his office at 424 Walnut Street in Philadelphia for group and individual sales and resided in the same city at 354 North Front Street.[13] The railroad typically scheduled all excursion trains to leave its Camden terminal at 6:30 a.m. or 7:00 a.m. (as shown in Figure 6). This not only provided the maximum amount of time for attendees to enjoy the sand, surf, and attractions offered in Atlantic City, but it also cleared the Camden and Atlantic's mainline for regular passenger and freight train service. The July 1865 Camden and Atlantic schedule called for excursion trains departing from the Atlantic City station at 5:18 p.m.

The Christian Recorder, previously cited above, carried the following advertisement for the excursion on its page 139 (Figure 7):

Advertisement.

FOR THE SEA SHORE.

A Grand Excursion

AND

Pic-nic to Atlantic City,

(For Colored Persons Exclusively.)

Will take place on TUESDAY, Sept. 5, 1865.

Fare going and returning: $1.25. Children under 10 years of age, 65 cts.

Tickets for sale at the Railroad Office, at the wharf, two hours before starting.

Last Boat leaves Vine St. Ferry at 6:30 A.M.

COMMITTEE OF ARRANGEMENTS.

JAMES W. PURNELL.	THOS. H. DORSEY.
HENRY JONES.	JOSHUA BROWN.
A.M. REILLY.	A. BERNARD.

O. DAVIS, S.C.

Figure 7. Advertisement for Grand Excursion, September 5, 1865.[14]

A number of the arrangement committee members involved in operating this excursion were men of means. Two of the men, Henry Jones and Thomas Dorsey (whose middle initial was actually "J.," indicating that the advertisement contains typos), were Philadelphia caterers of renown. W. E. B. Du Bois notes that

> … Dorsey was one of the triumvirate of colored caterers—the other two being Henry Jones and Henry Minton—who some years ago might have been said to rule the social world of Philadelphia through its stomach. Time was

when lobster salad, chicken croquettes, deviled crabs and terrapin composed the edible display at every big Philadelphia gathering, and none of those dishes were thought to be perfectly prepared unless they came from the hands of one of the three men named. Without making any invidious comparisons between those who were such masters of the gastronomic art, it can fairly be said that outside of his kitchen, Thomas J. Dorsey outranked the others. Although without schooling, he possessed a naturally refined instinct that led him to surround himself with both men and things of an elevating character. It was his proudest boast that at his table, in his Locust street residence, there had sat Charles Sumner, William Lloyd Garrison, John W. Forney, William D. Kelley, and Fred Douglass. . . . Yet Thomas Dorsey had been a slave; had been held in bondage by a Maryland planter. Nor did he escape from his fetters until he had reached a man's estate. He fled to this city [Philadelphia], but was apprehended and returned to his master. During his brief stay in Philadelphia, however, he made friends, and these raised a fund of sufficient proportion to purchase his freedom. As a caterer he quickly achieved both fame and fortune. His experience of the horrors of slavery had instilled him with an undying reverence for those champions of his down-trodden race, the old-time Abolitionists. He took a prominent part in all efforts to elevate his people, and in that way he came in close contact with Sumner, Garrison, Forney and others.[15]

Henry Jones was in the catering business for thirty years, and died September 24, 1873, leaving a considerable estate. Born in Virginia, Jones always approached his business engagements with a great sense of responsibility. He catered for families in Philadelphia, New Jersey and New York.[16]

Thomas J. Dorsey was the father of William Dorsey, Philadelphia's reputed first black historian and scrapbook compiler.[17] Roger Lane's work, *William Dorsey's Philadelphia & Ours: On the Past and Future of the Black City in America*, notes the following about the Dorsey family:

> William Henry Dorsey was born in 1837, the oldest child and only son of one of the most prominent members of Philadelphia's mid-19th-century black elite. His father, Thomas J., had escaped from slavery in Maryland before marrying Louise Tobias, a free woman from Pennsylvania, and establishing one of the leading catering firms in the city. The son, with his sisters Sarah and Mary Louise, grew up in a household increasingly used to the relative wealth and status conferred by this success story.[18]

Also listed in the advertisement was Alexander Bernard, who resided at 535 Callowhill Street in Philadelphia and operated a restaurant in the Quaker City.[19] Joshua Brown worked as a salesman and lived at 711 Lombard Street,[20] while A. M. Riley (*sic*) was a professional barber with two addresses: 198 S. 6th Street and 4341 Race Street in Philadelphia.[21] The identity of O. Davis, Special Counselor, is not clear, but he was likely Obadiah Davis, a black barber from South Camden.[22] Those who took advantage of this exclusive excursion for people of color most assuredly enjoyed sumptuous food with such auspicious caterers and restaurateurs involved.

Despite the excursion occurring in the off-season, the day's events went smoothly. A regular weekly summer column appearing in the pages of the *South Jersey Republican* for September 8, 1865, provides an earnest description of the excursion's events of three days prior:

OUR ATLANTIC CITY LETTER.
ATLANTIC CITY, *Sept.* 7, 1865.

Mr. Editor.—The past week at this place has been as oppressively hot as most of the weather in the summer, a few days which were absolutely "scorching." Though the bathing has been excellent, there have been few people here to enjoy it save those who have come on excursions, and they have been quite a feature of interest. On the 5th, the colored people came down, and although their number was small, they made decidedly a fine contrast to the rowdy crowds who had previously visited this place. They were orderly, not a single disturbance of any kind having occurred to mar their pleasure. Had it not been for their color, one would not have known but that it was the most respectable excursion of the season. Another, it is said, will come down on the 12th instant. A few strait-jacketed copperheads, who have the name of keeping hotels, refused to give them any accommodations, or to sell them anything at all; but to Mr. Elias Cleaver, of the Tammany House, belongs the credit and honor of giving to them many conveniences which they required.—Some men are so thin-skinned that they need a little color on them to make them sensible.[23]

TAMMANY HOUSE, ATLANTIC CITY, N. J. Elias Cleaver, the well-known caterer, has refitted his house, and is now ready for the reception of guests. The bar has been removed to the adjoining house, and a first-class barber shop added.
Meals surplied at any hour.

Figure 8. Advertisement for the Tammany House Hotel, June 22, 1871.[24]

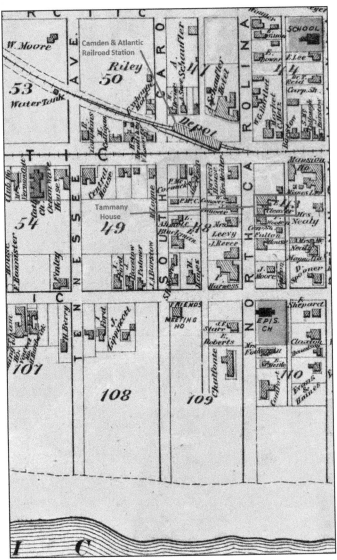

Figure 9. Detail from inset vignette map of Atlantic City, 1872.[25]

Mr. Elias Cleaver, detailed in the *South Jersey Republican* article above, was a white resident of Philadelphia who owned a catering business in the Quaker City, suggesting he was likely well acquainted with those who operated the excursion, providing him with further impetus to offer services to the group of African American revelers. A notice from the June 22, 1871, edition of *The Philadelphia Inquirer* confirms Cleaver's primary occupation as a city caterer of some renown (Figure 8).

An 1872 map detail (Figure 9) delineates the short distance between the Camden and Atlantic depot and the Tammany House Hotel, along with potentially identifying the other proximate hotels that discriminated and refused the excursionists any accommodation.

Although not expressly stated in the original advertisement or mentioned in the local follow-up article, presumably these African American day travelers used the hotel to don bathing garb and then trekked down North Carolina Avenue to the beach and surf, given the high temperatures that day (Figures 10 and 11).

HADDON HOUSE. LIPPINCOTT & STOKES, PROPR'S.
FOOT OF NORTH CAROLINA AVNE. ATLANTIC CITY, N.J.

Figure 10. The beach at the foot of North Carolina Avenue, Atlantic City, New Jersey, as it appeared in 1878.[26]

While the *South Jersey Republican* article cited before mentions that another excursion would operate a week later, no record of that trip has been found in various newspaper archives. Inclement weather or poor ticket sales might provide an explanation for the apparent lack of a second excursion during the 1865 season.

This excursion operated in September, as African Americans arriving at Atlantic City in groups of almost any size were summarily relegated to attend the resort after the summer months, the traditional season for white visitation. This practice changed somewhat during the later years of the nineteenth century to include days during the

NORTH CAROLINA AVENUE, LOOKING TOWARDS THE OCEAN FROM PACIFIC AVENUE.

Figure 11. North Carolina Avenue looking towards the beach, 1875.[27]

summer for people of color to visit the shore, although post-season September was prime time for blacks at the beach, as author Roger Lane notes,

> . . . by far the most important goal of Philadelphia's excursionists was the Jersey shore. Several members of the city's [Philadelphia] black elite owned their own summer homes in New Jersey, while employers complained that once the summer turned hot, domestics could not be kept from following the salt breezes to the east. Certain days, often Thursdays, the traditional maids' day off, were set aside as, for example, "Colored People's Salt Water Day" at resorts presumably segregated the rest of the week. Above all, Atlantic City, where many Philadelphians had family and other connections, offered an array of amusements regardless of weather. And while visitors flocked to the boardwalk at any time, it was recognized that September—a little past the season and so the monthly equivalent of Thursday—was special to Afro-Americans.[28]

CONCLUSION

Viewed as a singular event, the first black excursion to Atlantic City proved a great success, albeit the trip attracted only a small cadre of people. Were some of Philadelphia's African Americans afraid to test their new hard-won freedom? Or was it strictly the economics that kept would be revelers at home? These are intangibles that cannot be answered. Within a much wider scope, however, the Grand Excursion of September 1865 was among the first shots fired in a long-running battle to carve out a place for people of color to enjoy America's Playground, despite dealing with institutional racism from the beginning that only grew worse over time. Reconstruction and the post-reconstruction era brought many more black visitors to Atlantic City, with virtually all of them arriving by train. Numerous organizations sponsored many more black excursions with advertisements for these trips appearing in newspapers beginning in 1869. By the mid-1880s, the *State Journal*, a black newspaper published in Harrisburg, carried a regular column from Atlantic City during the summer months. Reading like a large city social column, the preparer would mention who had arrived in the city by the sea, where they were staying, and with whom they were socializing. It appears city officials and lifeguards began enforcing segregation among the ocean waves by the turn of the twentieth century. This discriminatory practice led to the establishment of the fully segregated "Chicken Bone Beach," located on the south side of Young's Million Dollar Pier at the foot of Missouri Avenue. Virtually all of the hotels, boarding houses, and cottages catering to an African American clientele stood within the Northside neighborhood, along with the businesses and night spots that black tourists required and enjoyed. Despite the animus the first black excursionists faced in 1865 at the hands of hotel keepers, none of them could have imagined how entrenched institutional racism would become in Atlantic City. After all, they only came for a day of eating, revelry, and bathing in what would become America's Playground.

Endnotes

Paul W. Schopp is the Assistant Director of the South Jersey Culture & History Center at Stockton University. He is a professional historian with over 42 years of experience working in the local history field. He is a well-known authority in the New Jersey history realm for his many reports, published articles, and books on state and Delaware Valley history. He is a member in long-standing of the West Jersey History Roundtable. For the past 25 years, Paul has conducted extensive research into South Jersey African American history.

1   Anonymous, "The Artizans' Excursion," *Daily Pennsylvanian* [Philadelphia], August 8, 1854, 2.

2   1860 Decennial Census, Population Schedules, Egg Harbor Township, Atlantic County, New Jersey, National Archives Microfilm Roll M653-682.

3   Anonymous, "Atlantic City," *The Christian Recorder* [Philadelphia], August 2, 1862, 122.

4   Federal Reserve Bank of Philadelphia, *Atlantic City: Past as Prologue: A Special Report by the Community Affairs Department* (Philadelphia: Federal Reserve Bank, 2009), 9.

5   Bryant Simon, *Boardwalk of Dreams: Atlantic City and the Fate of Urban America* (New York: Oxford University Press, 2004), 66.

6   "Union Cottage" advertisement, *The Christian Recorder*, August 2, 1862, 123.

7   "Excursion for Old Ocean!" advertisement, *Camden Democrat*, June 27, 1863, 3. 8

8   "Camden and Atlantic Railroad," *Ashcroft's Railway Directory for 1866* (New York: John Ashcroft, [1866]), 61.

9   "Election Returns," *Centinel of Freedom* [Newark], November 13, 1855, 1.

10 "Legislative," *Centinel of Freedom* [Newark], January 15, 1861, 4.

11 Anonymous, "The Excursion to Atlantic City," *The Christian Recorder*, September 2, 1865, 138.

12 "Camden and Atlantic Railroad," timetable, *Illustrated New Age* [Philadelphia], August 23, 1865, 4.

13 A. McElroy, *McElroy's Philadelphia City Directory for 1865 . . .* (Philadelphia: A. McElroy, 1865), 107.

14 "For the Sea Shore. A Grand Excursion," advertisement, *The Christian Recorder,* September 2, 1865, 139.

15 William Edward Burghardt Du Bois, *The Philadelphia Negro: A Social Study* (Philadelphia: The University of Pennsylvania, 1899), 34-35.

16 Du Bois, *The Philadelphia Negro: A Social Study*, 34-35.

17 *N.B.*: William Dorsey was a prolific scrapbook compiler, creating over 400 such books before his death. Cheyney University microfilmed many of these scrapbooks, although not all, and sent the original compilations to Penn State University for safekeeping. The microfilm is only accessible through Cheyney University in Cheyney, Pennsylvania.

18 Roger Lane, *William Dorsey's Philadelphia and Ours* (New York: Oxford University Press, 1991), 2.

19 A. McElroy, *McElroy's Philadelphia City Directory for 1865 . . .* (Philadelphia: A. McElroy, 1865), 75.

20 A. McElroy, *McElroy's Philadelphia City Directory for 1866 . . .* (Philadelphia: A. McElroy, 1866), 107.

21 A. McElroy, *McElroy's Philadelphia City Directory for 1864 . . .* (Philadelphia: A. McElroy, 1864), 623.

22 Francis A. Cassedy, *Cassedy's Camden City Directory for the Years 1865 – 1866 . . .* (Camden, NJ: Francis A. Cassedy, 1865), 129.

23 Anonymous, "Our Atlantic City Letter," *South Jersey Republican*, September 8, 1865, 3.

24 "Tammany House, Atlantic City, N.J." advertisement, *The Philadelphia Inquirer*, June 22, 1871, 5.

25 F. W. Beers, *Topographical Map of Atlantic Co., New Jersey* (New York: Beers, Comstock & Cline, 1872), inset vignette map of Atlantic City.

26 T. F. Rose and H.C. Woolman, *Historical and Biographical Atlas of the New Jersey Coast.* (Philadelphia: Woolman & Rose, 1878), 329.

27 Dr. Thomas K. Reed, "Atlantic City." Published in the June 1875 edition of *Godey's Lady Book* (Philadelphia: Louis Godey, 1875), 515.

28 Lane, *William Dorsey's Philadelphia*, 1991, 319-20.

Proving a Legend:
A Submarine in the Rancocas Creek

Alice Smith

In 1947, Barbara Frank, an eighth-grade student at Walnut Street School in Delanco, Burlington County, New Jersey, submitted her local history report concerning the lore of her hometown. In her report, Barbara included a story about a submarine in the waters of the Rancocas Creek around 1861.[1] About three decades after she wrote the report, researchers for an American bicentennial publication titled *The Delanco Story – Its Past and Present*, copied the submarine story from Barbara Frank's history paper, and included a bullet point about the event in a chapter titled "Potpourri," which covers personalities and legends. The committee explained that they did not verify the legends, but felt they were "worth repeating because maybe they did happen." The bullet point referencing the submarine reads:

> In 1861, a boat came up the creek and landed at the railroad bridge. It was called a diving boat and was built by a Frenchman. The Government sent officers from Washington and they had many trials of the boat, now called a submarine.[2]

Other than Barbara Frank's history report and its reiteration in *The Delanco Story – Its Past and Present* decades later, the legend of a submarine in the Rancocas River was never officially verified—or questioned, for that matter. In August 2004, Delanco resident Kevin McLaughlin shared an email with me that was forwarded to him by his brother, Timothy McLaughlin. Tim had retired from the U.S. Navy as a Lt. Commander in 1991, then obtaining a position as a civilian for the Military Sealift Command at the Washington Navy Yard. The email contained a Civil War-era letter sent to Captain Samuel F. DuPont at the U.S. Naval Station, Philadelphia, signed by Commander Henry K. Hoff, Commander Chas. Steadman and Chief Engineer Robert Danby.[3]

Dated July 7, 1861, the officers acknowledged DuPont's orders to examine a diving machine at Delanco, the invention of French engineer Brutus de Villeroi. The remainder of the letter describes the physical appearance of the submersible as an "iron cylinder, cone shaped at the two extremities, 33 feet in length, four feet at its greatest diameter, with 36 glass bull eyes on the back." The inspectors also recorded their findings about the vessel's propulsion system, noting its ability to "remain submerged for a length of time [15 minutes], with the crew leaving and returning to the boat while under water . . . breathing by means of a tube connected with the boat."[4]

On Thursday, June 20, 1861, the day of the submersible's trials, the creek "was rough, and the machinery was not of sufficient power to operate in satisfactory manner."[5] However, the lack of functionality that day did not stop the naval officers from concluding their letter with the following recommendation, proving the legend to be reality:

> That in the event of war, with a foreign power, the mere knowledge that we possessed such a mysterious invisible engine of destruction, would have the effect of producing great caution on the part of invading fleet in our waters, causing apprehension and alarm in the minds of those on board as to their safety while lying at anchor in a river or a roadstead.[6]

A front-page article appeared in the Saturday edition of *The Philadelphia Inquirer* on May 18, 1861,

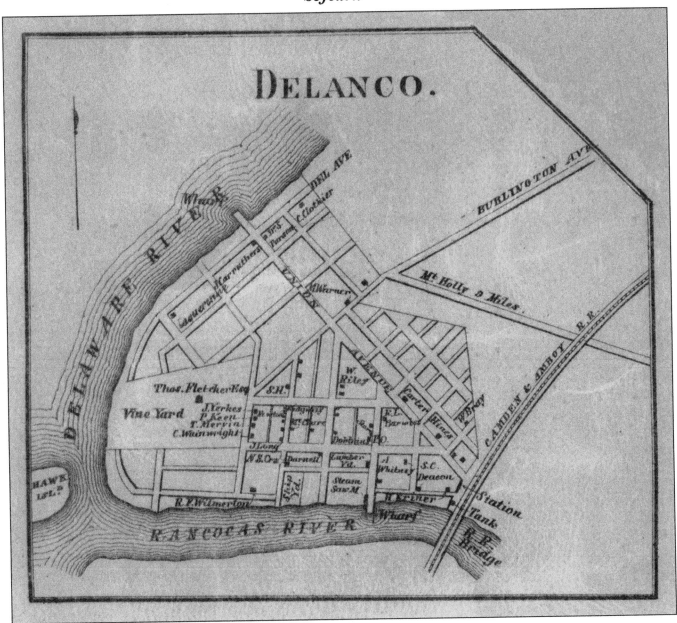

Delanco vignette map, detail, *New Map of Burlington County*, Parry, Sykes and Earl, 1859.

revealing the intentions of the naval observers who traveled to Delanco, as well as Mr. de Villeroi's own interest there.

Helping to safeguard a divided nation with circumspect ports since the First Battle of Fort Sumter in Charleston, the Philadelphia Harbor Police had seized de Villeroi's vessel in the Delaware River, arrested the crew, and chained the submersible to the Noble Street Pier. The *Inquirer's* reporter penned the excitement of the crowd as they watched from the pier to get a glimpse of what many believed to be a "monster."

Never since the days of the Battle of the Kegs has the river front of Philadelphia been the scene of such a peculiar excitement as yesterday. At an early hour in the morning rumors spread like wildfire among the inflammable population crowding our wharves that a monster, half aquatic, half aerial, and wholly incomprehensible, had been captured by Harbor Police, and had been safely chained at the foot of Noble street pier.

Forthwith the pier became the grand center of attraction. The crowds increased hourly, the spectators flocking to see the amphibious and ambiguous creature. All sorts of speculations were freely indulged in as to the uses and purposes of the lengthy iron circular continuance, all tending however, to the belief that it was designed to aid and assist JEFF. DAVIS in the benevolent occupation of transferring Federal vessels of war into flying morsels of wood and iron, i.e. blowing them up, while everyone concurred in the opinion that it was "very like a whale."

The monster itself, on a close inspection, proved to be a submarine propeller, invented by Monsieur DE VILLEROI, a French gentleman, who has devoted many years to experiments in this direction. The hull was built about two years ago, at the machine works of NEALL, MATTHEWS, & MOORE, on Bush Hill, and at that time was reputed to be under the joint ownership of its inventor and MR. GIRARD, a connection of the benefactor, and one of the claimants to his vast estates. In its unfinished condition it attracted the attention of the HON. WM. H. WITTE, who induced its removal to the Penn Iron Works of REANEY, NEAFIE & CO., where it was supplied with a propelling apparatus.[7]

The last two paragraphs of the article reveal the Rancocas Creek connection:

Since that time, the submarine vessel has for divers reasons been stationed in sundry places. Of these were Marcus Hook, New Castle, and Delanco on the Rancocas. A number of experiments were tried, with a view of adopting it to recovering goods from wrecks, and examining the bottoms of rivers, but from all that we can gather, the machine has proved an utter failure for all practical purposes.

The first information that the police had of the appearances of the vessel opposite our city, was that it was taking in a quantity of pig lead, which was to be used as ballast, in some experiments which were contemplated. At the time of its seizure it was under the charge of a young Frenchman, named ALEXANDER RHODES, and HENRY KRINER [Kreiner/Kriener], an American, were arrested. They stated that the machine was to be taken to the Navy Yard to be

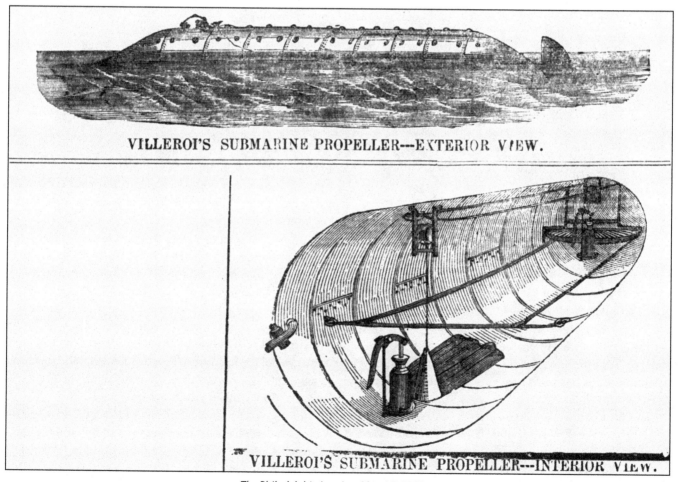

VILLEROI'S SUBMARINE PROPELLER---EXTERIOR VIEW.

VILLEROI'S SUBMARINE PROPELLER---INTERIOR VIEW.

The Philadelphia Inquirer, May 18, 1861, 1.

Lithograph of Reaney, Neafie, & Levy Shipyard, c. 1850.

examined by Government officers to ascertain whether it could be made serviceable in naval operations. Its movements and this intention have not been kept a secret, and at any other time than the present, no excitement would have been created by its appearance. We have no doubt that all connected with it will be able to explain the objects which were contemplated by its erratic movement in the waters.[8]

Researchers are still unable to determine if Monsieur de Villeroi concocted this cruise as a stunt to draw attention to his boat or if it was an actual river trial for distance and endurance.

Inventor Brutus de Villeroi arrived in New York in 1856 aboard the American ship Panama[9] from Bordeaux, France, with his wife Eulalie. Enumerated a year prior to the seizure of the submarine boat, the 1860 decennial census recorded that the couple resided in Philadelphia, Pennsylvania.[10] They also appear on a population schedule for Marcus Hook, Pennsylvania,[11] while staying at the Spread Eagle Hotel with the submarine crew. Written in the occupation column of de Villeroi's census entry are the words "natural genius."

Although a man of advanced years, sea travel did not appear to bother de Villeroi—he evidently made several trips between France and the United States, first arriving in Philadelphia as early as February 1849. In a cover letter to the Franklin Institute regarding the submission of a telescope invention, he lists his residency as 72 South 12th Street. The Institute awarded de Villeroi the John Scott Medal for his "ordinary telescope with an attached appendage" invention, seemingly warranting the Frenchman's "natural genius" proclamation.[12]

Following the demonstration at Delanco, Monsieur de Villeroi received a naval contract for $14,000 to build his submarine at the Neafie and Levy Shipyard in Philadelphia. The result, the Union's 47-foot submarine the USS Alligator, was launched on May 1, 1862. Unfortunately, Mother Nature thwarted de Villeroi's genius before the

A photograph of the Franklin Institute's John Scott Medal.

submersible ever served as a war machine for the Union. During a fierce storm in April 1863, the USS Alligator met her demise off the coast of Cape Hatteras after the captain of the USS Sumter, the vessel towing the USS Alligator, ordered the hawser pulling the submersible severed before she pulled the USS Sumter down with her.[13] The Confederate's submarine, the CSS Hunley, would not be commissioned until three months after the Alligator came to rest on the ocean floor in the Graveyard of the Atlantic, a stretch of sea surrounding the Outer Banks notorious for housing shipwrecks.

The USS Alligator is in the Graveyard of the Atlantic, but where is the prototype? Could she be buried where she trained in the marshlands along the Rancocas Creek?

Today's Search for the Prototype in the Rancocas

Upon further investigation into the prototype submarine's history, the names Alexander Rhodes and Henry Kriner—the two men arrested when port officials seized the submarine along the Philadelphia waterfront—place the crew in Delanco as early as 1859. Eighteen-year-old Delanco resident Henry Kriner was familiar with the Rancocas and Delaware waterways, since he worked as a wharf builder for his father. Alexander Rhodes was an émigré from France. After Brutus de Villeroi received the contract for the construction of a larger vessel, the Navy hired Rhodes in November 1861 to serve as an operative on the new Submarine Propeller. Rhodes' Civil War pension records acquaint us with the names of some additional crew members involved with the prototype. In December 2004, the pension records were searched and appropriate photocopies obtained:[14]

I [Rhodes] was on the machine from the time I came in this country in 1859 from [Bordeaux] France … where I had lived from birth. Landed at Philadelphia on board the Infernal Machine, or Torpedo Boat, at Philadelphia, and we came up to Rancocas Creek, near Delanco, where we

drilled. It had no name and was on it till late in 1862 and was then discharged at the Philadelphia Navy Yard … Cooper Woodington who was in the torpedo boat. He is at Bridgeboro, Bur. Co., N.J. and Peter Leon, Riverside, New Jersey. …

How long were you [Woodington] on the torpedo boat with him and how intimately did you know him [Rhodes] … From the spring of 1861 for about ten months. He was on her when I went aboard and had been for some time … I boarded at the same place, slept in the same room … I was discharged at Washington, D.C. … In spring or early summer of 1862 there were two torpedo boats. The first one I went on here was a small one which they experimented with. He was with me on her. I left her in June for five months and was off until spring of 1862 when in April, I think they sent for me to go on the large torpedo and he was mate aboard of this last one and in a few months when McClellan situated to Harrison's Landing, the crew was divided and he was left with the part of the crew that remained with the tug which went with the machine. … He was a short young fellow and always appeared in good health. He could hardly speak English at first.[15]

Peter Leon is essential to our modern search of the creek area for remnants of the prototype. According to a family letter from a Leon descendant, the cigar-shaped boat laid within the Rancocas Creek or its adjoining mudflats at Riverside for several years.[16] No documentation exists at this time to prove that the prototype ever departed from the Rancocas Creek area.

The search for the submarine prototype began in spring 2004 with an attempt to access the marsh area along the creek from Harrison Street, Riverside. The marsh area proved treacherous, with little firm footing or enough support for a person's weight.

On July 30, 2005, our submarine search crew departed Paul Manion's ramp on the Delanco side of the creek at 9 a.m., several hours after low tide. The crew consisted of Ed Colimore, a reporter with *The Philadelphia Inquirer*, April Saul, Colimore's photographer, kayaker Bob Donahue, and local residents Richard Pattanite, Linda Tusing and Peter Fritz. It was a beautiful day on the Rancocas, but the tide was higher than expected and we could not enter the marsh. The area in question has four ditches, with the fourth ditch being the widest. Both Pattanite and Joe D'Agostino expressed that the fourth ditch was where they remembered seeing the rusted hull. Later that day, I spoke with Emerson Lucas who divulged that Bob Barnett and his family swam in the ditches, and that Barnett heard the story about a submarine buried in the ditch. We planned to make another excursion in late fall, when we could enter the marsh on foot from Harrison Street.

While kayaking in the ditch areas that November, Bob Donahue and Nancy Mason discovered a suspicious mound. President of Black Laser Learning and remote-sensing expert Vince Capone arrived a month later with the necessary equipment to conduct a scientific search. Using a Marine Magnetic Explorer and a survey-grade Trimble GPS system, Capone merged the data from both units via the HYPACK survey software running on a laptop computer, which would determine if the mound contained ferrous material. The outcome proved that the magnetometer reading at the mound was too low to be the prototype.

Bob Donahue stands on the mound he discovered in November 2005.

In November 2007, another search excursion utilizing a twenty-two foot boat departed from Lightning Jack's marina at 11:15 a.m. under the leadership of Vince Capone, Charles "Chuck" Rhine, and Craig Ulrich from Enviroscan, Inc. The magnetometer identified two potential targets: one at the marine railway that extended across the Riverside marsh area and another further down the creek. The boat left the creek about 2:30 p.m and the crew reviewed the magnetometer readings along side the side-scan sonar images. The sonar results yielded no images of the submarine and the magnetometer readings proved to be too high, prompting the question: did de Villeroi dump pig iron in his submarine to keep it submerged and hidden?

In January 2009, a boat crewed by Captain Bob Marshall and Assistant Sonar Technician Justin McKinley left the wharf area at 9:15 a.m. with sonar equipment on board, and a scan of the area near Hawk Island Marina revealed a high volume of debris in the creek. A subsequent evaluation of the sonar results identified several suspicious sites, but yielded no concrete evidence.

Vince Capone fine tunes his instrument on the boat in preparation for the submarine search.

Vince Capone departed Hawk Island Marina at 9:20 a.m. on June 7, 2011, with diver Mike Fletcher and Sonar Technician McKinley. The magnetometer proved unreliable that day, but the crew still searched the marsh area. However, they did not find any remnants of the bulkhead or the submarine. The technicians dispatched the maps to Vince Capone for further investigation. In 2012, Vince Capone, Steve Gatto, and Justin McKinley tested the new Hummingbird Sonar equipment. After hours on the creek, a text message sent to the author read, "No Joy."

Frank Astemborski remembered ghastly tales that the older boys told, scaring him into believing that dead men lay hidden inside a strange hull that they found partly submerged in the Riverside marsh. He remembered peering reluctantly through the glass windows to get a glimpse of the remains. Bud Eldridge remembered seeing a submarine hatch. Richard Pattanite leaped from a rope swing and landed on a rusted metal hull. He scrambled to safety as the iron vessel disintegrated beneath his weight.

At times it feels as if we are imaginary characters living in a type of Goldilocks's fairytale, with the magnetometer readings being too high or too low and not "just right" for properly identifying the submarine's location. The Rancocas Creek is holding onto its secrets. Mssrs. Astemborski and Eldridge are no longer with us; will their factual recollections become the lifespring of new legends among our youth? Only time will tell.

ENDNOTES

Mrs. Alice M. Smith, a local historian, has lived in the triple-town area of Delanco, Riverside, and Delran for over sixty-nine years. As the current historian for the Dobbins Memorial United Methodist Church in Delanco, Alice completed a five-year research project which culminated with the publication of a book titled *A Sermon in Glass*, published in 2003. For the past eight years, she has served as the President of the Riverside Historical Society and conducted research for Riverside's history book—*Riverside, New Jersey: 150 Years of Progress, 1851 – 2001.*

Her current project is the *Hunt for the USS Alligator – the Union's Civil War Submarine*. In 2005, she was an invited guest speaker at the National Oceanic and Atmospheric Administration's (NOAA) Third Annual Alligator Symposium and Workshop, held at the Independence Seaport Museum in Philadelphia. Her presentation centered on local research—hunting for descendants of the submarine's crew and the submarine prototype, which, according to the descendants of Pierre Leon's family, may still be in the waters of the Rancocas Creek along Riverside's shore. Contact Alice at delancoalice@hotmail.com.

1   Personal Communication, Barbara Frank Page, 2004. During a telephone conversation with Barbara, she revealed the source she used while writing her history report. It was the diary of Andress Ridgway (1833 – 1926), who operated the local shoe factory in Delanco. At this writing, the location of the Ridgway diary is unknown.

2   Charles A. Frush, et al, eds., *The Delanco Story – Its Past and Present* (Delanco, NJ: The Delanco Bicentennial Book Committee, 1977), 124.

3   NARA Record Group (RG) no. 71, Bureau of Yards and Docks, letters sent and received, 1861 – 1863. National Archives and Records Administration, Washington, D.C.

4   "The Submarine Propeller," *The Philadelphia Inquirer*, June 25, 1861, 8.

5   Ibid.

6   NARA, RG 71.

7   "The Seizure of Villeroi's Submarine Propeller," *The Philadelphia Inquirer*, Saturday, May 18, 1861, 1. "The Battle of the Kegs" refers to an attack on January 5, 1778, against the British fleet at Philadelphia. David Bushnell, inventor of the submersible Turtle, left Bordentown, New Jersey, on a ebbing tide. He dropped floated explosive kegs of gunpowder into the Delaware River, hoping to harass shipping and incapacitate the British fleet in Philadelphia Harbor. Although a number of curious youths in a rowboat lost their lives, little damage occurred to shipping. Francis Hopkinson memorialized the event in a patriotic ballad.

8   Ibid.

9   New York Arrivals 1851-1891, Roll 177, p. 6, List 992. LDS Valley Forge Stake, Family History Center. Ancestry.com—Credit: researcher Dan Cashin.

10 1860 federal decennial census, Philadelphia, Pennsylvania, 7th Ward, June 11, 1860, Roll 1157, 553.

11 1860 federal decennial census, Lower Chichester Township, Marcus Hook, Delaware County, June 9, 1860, Roll 1105, 254.

12 A. Michal McMahon and Stephanie A. Morris, *Technology in Industrial America: The Committee on Science and the Arts of the Franklin Institute, 1824 – 1900*, Wilmington, DE: SR Scholarly Resources Inc., 1977, 68.

13 "The Navy – The Submarine Battery Alligator," *New York Herald*, April 15, 1863, 10.

14 NARA, Civil War Pension papers pertaining to pensioner Rose Rhodes, widow of Alexander Rhodes, Cert. No. 918757.

15 NARA, Deposition, Case of Alexander Rhodes, No. 7109.

16 Letter written by Chet Bucher, son of Henrietta Leon Bucher, to Emily and Pete Leon. Henrietta Leon was the daughter of Pierre Leon, 1984.

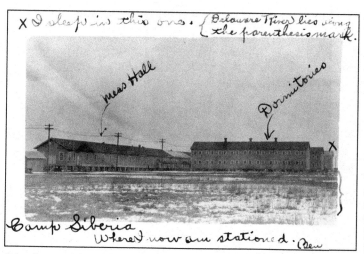

Camp Pedricktown. Ben, the sender of this postcard, called this bleak installation, "Camp Siberia." The only site reference is the proximate Delaware River. It took quite a bit of sleuthing to determine that this image, from the winter of 1918 – 1919, shows the earliest iteration of Camp Pedricktown, the supply depot constructed for the Delaware Ordnance District. In September 1918, the federal government informed a group of farmers who owned 2,000 acres along the Delaware in Oldmans Township, that their property would be confiscated for a new military facility. The new post would include a large storage facility for explosive powder to be shipped to the European War Theatre of operations. The government asked the local residents to provide room and board for the hundreds of workers who would arrive to build the installation. After the war ended, the Delaware Ordnance District maintained its presence at the base through 1958. During the Cold War, from 1960 – 1966, Pedricktown became a Nike Missile Master Installation and a key radar facility with the Army Air Defense Command and headquarters for the 42nd and 43rd Artillery. Other Army units came and went from the late 1960s until the 1990s, when the Base Realignment and Closure Commission shuttered the base.

New Editions of Books about the Still Family of South Jersey

Levin and Charity Still were born in Maryland as slaves in the second half of the eighteenth century. Levin bought his freedom and together with Charity, who escaped her bondage, they raised a remarkable family in the Pine Barrens of South Jersey. The lives of three of their children—James, William, and Peter—have been memorialized in print. The South Jersey Culture & History Center has reprinted two of these texts; republication of the third is underway.

Early Recollections and Life of Dr. James Still

During the nineteenth century, James Still was perhaps the most gifted physician in South Jersey. He was an African American son of former slaves, who received no more than six months of traditional schooling, and was self taught in both medical knowledge and practice. Born in Washington Township, Burlington County, New Jersey (now Shamong), Dr. Still overcame poverty and racial animus to

become one of the wealthiest men in South Jersey during his lifetime. This republication of his outstanding autobiography, self-published in 1877, is a stirring reminder of the power of self-determination and faith.

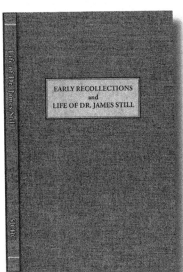

This new edition of *Early Recollections* is not a facsimile reproduction but is newly typeset with foreword by Samuel C. Still III and introduction by Paul W. Schopp. This edition also includes a new and enlarged index.
179 pages, paperback
ISBN: 978-0-9888731-6-2
$8.95

William Still: His Life and Work to This Time by James P. Boyd

Known as the Father of the Underground Railroad for his efforts in moving fugitive enslaved Africans while recording their harrowing stories, William Still lived a life dedicated to the betterment of all mankind during the dark days of American slavery. His book *The Underground Rail Road*, first published in 1872, provides a first-hand account of the tribulations faced by those seeking to live free from bondage. Born in Shamong, Burlington County, New Jersey, during 1821, William was the son of slaves, which provided him with the impetus to aid others. His faith and determination made

him an extraordinary man whose life is worthy of study.

This is a republication of James P. Boyd's 1886 life of William Still. Included are selections from Still's *The Underground Rail Road* that shed further light on his life and times. Foreword by Samuel C. Still III. Includes index.
211 pages, paperback
ISBN: 978-0-997699-5-4

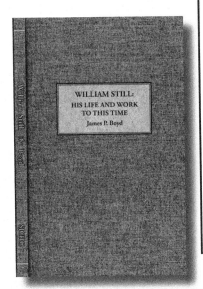

A new edition of Kate E. R. Pickard's *The Kidnapped and the Ransomed*, originally published in 1856, is underway. It documents the harrowing recollections of Peter Still and his wife Vina, who spent forty years in slavery before being reunited with the Still family in South Jersey.

Brevet Brigadier General Elias Wright:
Surveyor Extraordinaire

Elizabeth G. Carpenter

Obituaries: their very placement within a hometown newspaper is noteworthy. A front-page obituary identifies the deceased as a person of prominence. In the early twentieth century, this special coverage was most often reserved for men of local distinction. Such was the case for Brevet Brigadier General Elias Wright, whose hometown newspaper, the *Daily Evening Union* of Atlantic City, carried front-page stories on three separate days—January 2, 1901; January 3, 1901; and January 7, 1901—that detailed his life, his death, and his burial.[1]

Newspaper article titles also provide clues to the ways a community viewed the deceased. On January 3rd, the subtitle read, "A Serious Man and Useful Citizen Gained a Fortune." Reading further, it is reported that "His wife, Julia Ashley, who is a sister of Deputy Sheriff Leonard Ashley, and one daughter, an only child, survived him." Julia was the older sister to Leonard Ashley; they were descendants of the well-regarded Blackman family of Port Republic. The fortune Wright left was reputed to

Captain, later Brevet Brigadier General, Elias Wright (June 22, 1830 – January 2, 1901). *Courtesy United States Army Heritage & Education Center, Carlisle, Pennsylvania.*

be $100,000, the equivalent of nearly $3,000,000 in 2016.[2] The January 3 obituary continues, noting that "He owned considerable real estate in this city [Atlantic City] and personal property." It adds, "General Wright was an expert on titles and real estate records. Those of the Wharton estate he traced back to the king, bringing all the transfers down to date." But Wright was more than a humble surveyor.

On January 7, the day of his burial in Pleasantville's Greenwood Cemetery, the *Daily Evening Union* included the fact that comrades from General Joseph Hooker Post 32 of the Grand Army of the Republic escorted the General's body to the grave. The significance that the Civil War played in Wright's life was not only underscored by the soldiers who attended his funeral but also by the paper's observation that "a badge of the Loyal Legion was placed over his heart." Wright's active and ambitious spirit transcended his military career and followed him into his post-war life. An article subtitle stated that "He Spent Half a Century in This City and County Doing Work That

Lives after Him." It concludes with the thought that "He was painstaking and thorough in whatever he had to do."

The news of Wright's death held significance further than his home state of New Jersey. *The Philadelphia Inquirer* also mentioned the General in an obituary subtitled "He Was a Noted Civil War Veteran and Seashore Pioneer."[3] Various other papers in other locations carried similar brief obituaries, including the *New York Tribune*, *The Washington* [D.C.] *Times*, the *Boston Journal*, the *Springfield* [Massachusetts] *Republican*, and the Harrisburg *Pennsylvania Patriot*.

Where did this remarkable man come from? Mary Isabel Gibson Cone, Wright's descendant and an editor of *One Line of the Wright Family*, provides today's historians and genealogists with a "roadmap" to his early life, as well as to his later accomplishments.[4]

Elias was the grandson of George Wright Jr., a Revolutionary War veteran who resettled his family from Saybrooke, Connecticut, to Durham, Greene County, New York, at the war's conclusion. Elias' father, Anson, was the second child of George Junior and Elizabeth Post Wright. Anson was a veteran of the War of 1812. He and his wife, Abigail, established their farm along today's Route 67, known locally as Wright Street.[5] Reportedly, Elias, the seventh of their nine children, was diligent in his family's farm responsibilities; however, his lack of interest in education became a source of family frustration. By age twelve, he could barely read and was considered by many to be a dolt.[6]

Perhaps in part because of his son's challenging reputation for being slow, Anson Wright established a school in his own home. Mary Ann, Elias' sister who was ten years his senior, served as his teacher. Elias not only learned how to read and write, but showed an aptitude for mathematics, a skill that would serve him well as an adult.[7]

Elias' entrepreneurial spirit blossomed in his late teens. In 1848, just a few weeks shy of his eighteenth birthday, Anson gave his son permission to apprentice himself to his uncle, Joseph B. Purington, a master carpenter.[8] Elias worked at his trade in Greene and Albany counties, as well as the cities of Hudson, New York, and Bridgeport, Connecticut. In 1849, he attended Hiram Boucher's Private School in Hudson, where he continued his studies in mathematics.[9]

With his apprenticeship complete, Elias traveled south during the winters of 1851 and 1852 to study at his eldest brother Calvin's school in Williamstown, New Jersey.[10] To get from Durham to Williamstown, Elias needed a reliable north – south route. A packet boat sailing from the wharf at Catskill on the Hudson River, moving south to New York City then on to the bustling coastal community of Port Republic, New Jersey, may well have been his preferred mode of transportation. As Harriet S. Sander notes in her booklet, *Sketches of Old Port Republic*, this was "considered the safest harbor between New York and Baltimore."[11]

Upon arriving at Port Republic, Wright might well have rested at The Franklin Inn, overlooking the mill pond and Nacote Creek, before taking a stage to Williamstown. This possible stop-over would have given him time to meet local residents like the Blackmans and the Ashleys, well known as "pillars" of the community. The 1850 United States Census identifies Ralph Ashley and Sarah Blackman, his wife, as parents of seventeen-year-old Julia, the young woman who would become Elias' wife.

The Franklin Inn and Store, Mill Road, Port Republic, is now a private residence, March 2017. *From the author's collection.*

Both the Franklin Inn and what was once an adjacent store remain standing today. The Franklin Inn was erected about 1778, while the brick store was constructed a decade later. Mr. Daniel Knauer, a contractor and builder from Atlantic City, acquired the property in 1936. As historians from the Historic American Buildings Survey wrote in 1940, Mr. Knauer, "restored and connected them (the Inn and store) to compose one large residence."[12]

Once under his brother Calvin's able tutelage, Elias' proficiency in math increased. His overall scholarship improved, equipping him to accept a year-long teaching post in Leedsville, now Linwood, in Atlantic County. When this school year ended, he returned to New York State in 1853 to attend Reverend Alonzo Flack's

Seminary in Charlotteville, west of Albany.[13] Affiliated with the Methodist Episcopal Church, it opened in 1849 with Flack as principal. "Its heyday was in 1854 with 1,000 students registered."[14] Within a year, the once lackluster student returned to Atlantic County to teach, married Julia Ashley on September 17, 1855, and, as noted in Harriet Sander's *Sketches*, settled in Port Republic.

Oscar F. Benjamin, a Historic American Building Survey research editor, completed his search of land titles and probate records of Gloucester and Atlantic counties in August 1940, and compiled a report that provides a detailed timeline for the "life" of the Franklin Inn. This report connects the inn and store to Stephen Colwell, of Weymouth Furnace fame in Gloucester County, and, in turn, to Elias Wright.

By deed of 1st November 1856, Stephen Colwell and wife Sarah B. of Philadelphia conveyed to Elias Wright of Galloway, Atlantic County,* New Jersey, "First all that land and premises which was conveyed to Jonas Miller by three separate deeds, two from Obadiah Huntley, one dated 9 June 1827 and one dated 4 April 1828, the other deed from under the hand of Daniel Mathis dated 27 April 1824, containing 3.55 aces more or less, and from Jonas Miller the same descended by diverse good conveyances unto the aforesaid Stephen Colwell.

*This village in Galloway Twp. was known successively as Gravely Run, Wrangleborough, Unionville and Port Republic. Atlantic County was created in 1837 from parts of Gloucester.[15]

According to Benjamin's research, sixteen days later, on November 17, 1856, Elias Wright conveyed this property to his mother-in-law, Sarah Ashley, for $1,600.00, or the equivalent of $43,384.95 in 2016.[16] This sale included "one wharf situated on a ditch leading into Nacott Creek," a convenience that underscored the importance of waterway access to this seafaring community. The property remained within the Ashley family for the next eighty years, until 1936, when Daniel Knauer

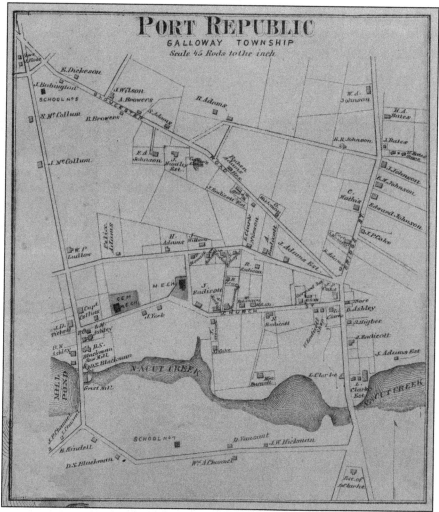

Vignette map of Port Republic, *Topographical Map of Atlantic Co., New Jersey: from Recent and Actual Surveys*, published by Beers, Comstock, Cline, 36 Vesey St., New York, 1872.

purchased it. A close examination of the 1872 Beers map (above) shows the R. M. Ashley property adjacent to Mill Pond. "R. M." was Rollin Mallory Ashley, Sarah's son and an older brother of Julia.

The late 1850s found Elias surveying land belonging to Stephen Colwell that, as Cone writes, included Egg Harbor City and the adjoining farms, totaling altogether 30,000 acres. Additionally, Elias "ran a line" for a railroad from Egg Harbor City to Mays Landing. Amid all this activity, he and Julia became parents of Frances, born on July 14, 1858.

On April 12, 1861, the Confederate firing on Fort Sumter signaled not only the beginning of the Civil War, but an interruption of the young family's life and Elias' surveying career. His military service began later that year when he recruited a state militia company from men living in today's Atlantic City area. After the First Battle of Bull Run, he led these men to Camden, then Trenton, where he was mustered in as Second Lieutenant of Company G, Fourth Regiment, New Jersey Volunteer Infantry, one of four regiments that formed New Jersey's

First Brigade.[17] Over the next four years, he moved up through the ranks, leading his men onto many fields of battle, including Gaines Mills, Fredericksburg, Chancellorsville, Salem Heights, Petersburg, Richmond, and ultimately the Battle of Fort Fisher on North Carolina's Cape Fear peninsula. This was followed by the trek up the peninsula to defeat Wilmington, the last haven for Confederate blockade runners.

After the Fredericksburg struggle, Elias was promoted to Captain, Company A, Fourth Regiment "for gallantry upon the field."[18] Not long after this, General William Birney tapped Captain Wright to raise and organize the first regiment of colored troops at Mason's Island in the District of Columbia.

White Officers always commanded United States Colored Troops. *Come and Join Us Brothers, by the Supervisory Committee For Recruiting Colored Regiments (1865). Image from Wikipedia.*

Wright was promoted to Major, First United States Colored Troops (USCT) Infantry, on June 24, 1863. After participating in the siege of Petersburg and Richmond, Wright was promoted to Lieutenant Colonel on the April 29, 1864. Four months later, he was again promoted, this time to Colonel of the Tenth USCT, an infantry unit that became part of the Twenty-fifth Army Corps assigned to the Army of the James.[19]

Not long after the defeat of Fort Fisher on January 15, 1865, Colonel Wright, now brevetted Brigadier General, led the Third Brigade, the Third Division of this Corps, in the Union's advance toward and ultimate defeat of Wilmington. During this desperate struggle, Wright was severely wounded in his right forearm by a musket ball, an injury that would plague him for the rest of his life. Despite this injury, Brevet Brigadier General Wright was present at the surrender of Confederate General Joseph E. Johnston at the Bennett House near Durham Station, North Carolina, on April 26, 1865.[20]

On May 31, 1865, General Wright tendered his resignation from the Union Army writing, "Having served nearly four years in the war my business as a civilian and pecuniary interest have been neglected for that length of time and now require my personal attention."[21] Brigadier General Charles Jackson Paine granted his approval of this request writing, in part, "He [Wright] is an eminently deserving officer, and now that the war is ended, is in my opinion entitled to claim consideration for his own interests."[22]

His resignation officially accepted, General Wright, as he came to be known, returned to South Jersey, to Julia, to daughter Frances, and to renewed employment with Stephen Colwell at the Weymouth tract. The 1866 edition of *Talbot & Blood's Business Directory of the State of New Jersey* lists him as "Agent, Real Estate" as well as "Engineer, Civil."[23]

In addition to clearing titles and surveying the land holdings of Stephen Colwell, the General's commitment to the development of Elwood became increasingly apparent. This included his leadership of the community's newly formed Grand Army of the Republic Post, an organization founded on the principles of fraternity, charity, and loyalty. A small article in the Saturday, September 26, 1868, edition of *The New Republic*, page 6, reported:

> G.A.R.—New Post Organized.—Capt. R. H. Lee, Junior Vice Grand Commander, of this State, organized a Post of that excellent beneficial and patriotic order, the Grand Army of the Republic, at Elwood, on Wednesday night. General Wright was elected Post Commander.

About a year later, on October 16, 1869, this same journal carried an article titled "A Visit to Atlantic County. What I Saw There." The writer devoted two paragraphs to Elwood:

> Elwood, in the township of Mullica, contains about 1,400 inhabitants, and is on the high road to wealth and prosperity.
>
> The place contains a ladies' boot and shoe factory, which is doing well, and will do better, as soon as the facilities are increased. The association is known as the Elwood Shoe Co. Geo. W. Rich is president, and General Elias Wright, Secretary.[24]

The 1870 United States Federal Census shows Elias, Julia, and Francis (nicknamed Frank), living in Mullica

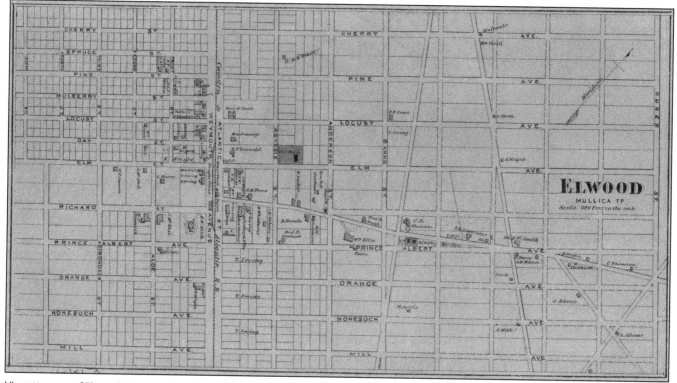

Vignette map of Elwood, *Topographical Map of Atlantic Co., New Jersey: from Recent and Actual Surveys*, published by Beers, Comstock, Cline, 36 Vesey St., New York, 1872.

Township. Wright's occupation was listed as Civil Engineer. The value of the family's real estate holdings was estimated to be $500.00, the equivalent of $9,630.70 in 2016, and the value of their personal property was estimated to be $15,000, the equivalent of $288,921.03 in 2016.[25] The Shoe Factory, situated near Richards Avenue, about a block from the Camden and Atlantic Railroad's Depot, appeared to be lucrative, as was his ownership of the steam sawmill, located at the corner of Orange Avenue and the rail line.[26] Further study of the Beers map vignette (above) suggests that Wright hoped this community, like neighboring Hammonton and Egg Harbor City, would have a significant agricultural component. Avenue names including Agricultural, Blackberry, Cranberry, Mulberry, Cherry, Orange, and Floral hint at this.

Around this time, Mary Ann Wright and her husband, William Ham, moved from Preble, Cortland County, New York, to Elwood. William was a farmer in Preble, while Mary Ann had enjoyed a sixteen-year teaching career that began years before when she patiently tutored twelve-year-old Elias. Both Mary Ann and William brought needed skills to the young community. Sadly, William died on June 16, 1876, about a decade after their move. William is buried in Laurel Hill Cemetery, situated at 1407 Elwood Road in Mullica Township, on the way to Pleasant Mills.[27]

Deeds tell stories: one dated December 13, 1876, reveals the creation of Laurel Hill Cemetery. This indenture records a land sale by Mary A. Ham, Executrix of the estate of William Ham, and by Elias Wright to the Laurel Hill Cemetery Association of Elwood "in consideration of the sum of One Dollar."[28] The property, "containing two acres and thirty nine one hundredth of an acre," was adjacent to the Ham farm. As the years passed, this quiet grove became the resting place for Elias' daughter, Frances, her husband, Benjamin Franklin Sooy, and their infant daughter, Julia Wright Sooy. Here also is buried Elias' younger sister, Ellen, her first husband, Peter Tilton Frambes, and two of their children, Bradford and Maybelle.

Not far from Elwood, other significant changes were taking place in 1876. Joseph Wharton, a Philadelphia resident and major industrialist who had long held an interest in New Jersey's Pine Barrens, purchased the Village of Batsto in 1876. Wharton was a man of grand plans who had the ability to surround himself with capable staff. Now he needed someone who not only had an agricultural background,

Frambes Monument in Mullica Township's Laurel Hill Cemetery. *From the author's collection.*

but was an experienced surveyor and land agent. He undoubtedly had heard from his friend Stephen Colwell, who died in 1871, that Elias Wright had served him well in these capacities at Weymouth. Wharton realized that this was the person he needed to hire.

A major order of business was the stabilization and renovation of the crumbling Richard's home at Batsto, a glorified farmhouse dating back to the mid-eighteenth century. Then came the first of several agricultural experiments, which included sugar-beet cultivation. The goal of such cultivation was to make half-refined syrup taken directly from beet roots. As Wharton explained to distinguished guests, including Professor George H. Cook, State Geologist of New Jersey; Dr. McMurtrie, of the Department of Agriculture, Washington, D.C.; Professor Frazer, of the Pennsylvania State Geological Survey, and others who journeyed with him from Philadelphia via the Camden & Atlantic Railroad, he wanted to determine "whether the beet root sugar industry, so important in France, Germany and other portions of Europe, can be profitably established in this country."[29] The group traveled by carriages from the Elwood Station to Batsto, "an ancient settlement in the lower part of Burlington county, and about six miles from Elwood."[30] While viewing the fifteen-acre experimental plot, the men listened to Mr. H. C. Humphrey, a chemist and overseer of the experiment, explain the process. After this, the group gathered at the mansion for dinner, then returned by train to Philadelphia.

Two months after this meeting, Joseph Wharton had a document printed that he titled "Proposals to Purchase Sugar Beets." The initial sentence of this proposal stated that "in order to test more fully the fitness of Jersey soil for sugar beet culture, I propose to contract with land owners in the vicinity of Batsto, Hammonton, Elwood, and Egg Harbor, for the purchase in 1878, of as many sugar beets as can be worked up at my Batsto mill, beyond my own crop. . . ." Potential participants were instructed to "lodge with my agent, Gen'l E. Wright, at Elwood, N. J., before Feb'y 20th, 1878, an application filled upon the blank at the foot of this notice." Further, farmers were told that their applications would be considered on a first come, first serve basis.[31] While the sugar beet experiment failed to produce the desired results, restoration of the mansion with its surrounding outbuildings proceeded nicely under the guidance of General Wright.

Not easily discouraged, Wharton investigated other possible agricultural activities, including the raising of heifers and cows, cranberry cultivation, and the harvesting of Menhaden, a fish species abundant along the New Jersey coast that could be used as fertilizer.[32] Only cranberry cultivation proved financially successful.

Although most of these agricultural ventures failed to produce sufficient revenue, Wharton, through Wright's surveying and title clearing efforts, continued to expand his holdings. Surveying in this pine-oak forest, with an often thick understory of scrub, demanded a well-organized team directed by the General. Axmen had to clear the way so chainmen could measure out the land and accurate measurements could be made, a task that required a mastery of trigonometry.[33]

During the 1880s and 1890s, relatives of Wright moved to Batsto to serve as superintendents of Wharton's farm. George Wright, an elder brother of the General's, served in this capacity from 1882 until his retirement in 1893. Then, Alonzo Norton, one of the General's nephews by marriage, continued in this position.[34]

United State Census Records for 1890 show General and Mrs. Wright residing at 24 North Pennsylvania Avenue, Atlantic City, New Jersey. His occupation is listed as "Architect." While his title searching and surveying efforts continued for Wharton, he became involved in Atlantic City as well as New Jersey planning efforts. In 1890, *The Times,* a Philadelphia newspaper, reported that General Elias Wright was one of three commissioners charged with "condemning of the sixty-foot strip of

Renovated Richards home, now Batsto Mansion, side view. *From the author's collection.*

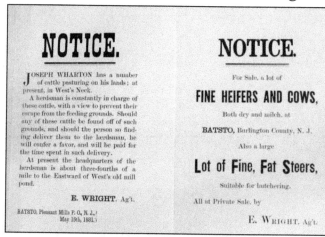

Image courtesy of New Jersey State Archives.

beach on which the new board-walk is to be constructed."[35] Later that year, a brief article in *The Philadelphia Inquirer* noted that the "Risley Lake Type Setting and Composing Machine Company" was again in operation in a new factory that is under the guidance of officers and financiers including vice president, Senator John J. Gardner of Egg Harbor and treasurer, Elias Wright, of Atlantic City.[36]

Tenacity, coupled with his sense of justice, prompted Wright to carry a tax-relief case to the State Supreme Court as reported in *The Philadelphia Inquirer*.[37] This action was prompted when the Commissioners of Appeal refused to reduce the assessment on 2,500 acres of land Wright owned in Galloway township.

A month after contesting this tax assessment, Wright was listed as a participant in a road improvement convention to be held at the State House in Trenton. His presentation was titled "The Location and Building of Roads," a topic for which he was well qualified, given his surveying expertise.[38]

A sampling of the General's Atlantic City land transactions during the final decade of the nineteenth century reveals substantial profits. On December 21, 1895, Wright and his wife, Julia, sold a lot to the Chelsea Branch Railroad Company. They received $1,200.00 for this transaction, the equivalent of $35,094 in 2016.[39] About four years later, on August 30, 1899, the General and Julia joined John J. Gardner and his wife, Mittie, in the sale of land to The Ventnor Dredging Company which garnered the sellers $400.00, the equiv-alent of $11,698 in 2016.[40]

Meanwhile, life on the western side of the Delaware River in Philadelphia grew increasingly difficult. Without a reliable source of clean drinking water, disease—at this time typhoid—was spreading. On January 21, 1898, *The Daily Union* carried an article titled "Philadelphia's Typhoid Epidemic" that declared:

The epidemic of typhoid fever in the northwestern section of the city has become so alarming that council yesterday considered a resolution that the secretary of the treasury be asked to send the surgeon general here to examine the water of the Schuylkill river and the Queen Lane reservoir, the chief sources of supply for the infected district. There was some opposition to the measure, and after debate it was referred to the health committee. There have been 366 new cases reported during the past two weeks.[41]

A year later, *The Philadelphia Inquirer* ran an article, complete with a map titled "Suggested Water-Shed in South Jersey," that proposed a solution. The article's lead sentence underscored exactly what Joseph Wharton had proposed earlier: "The fact that there is a supply of virgin pure water lying almost at the doors of Philadelphia, in the pine woods of Southern New Jersey, which, if pushed to its limit, will furnish as much as one thousand million gallons a day, has been brought to the attention of the city authorities." The next sentence reflected the reception Wharton's idea had received from Philadelphia's city fathers in 1891: "With characteristic indifference on all that concerns the water problems, however, the administration has shelved this in company with every other plan proposed for the betterment of increase of the city's supply."[42]

Without the careful title searching and expert surveying of Elias Wright, such a proposal would not have been possible. With his reputation for accuracy and fair dealing, it is not surprising that Wright presided at the annual session of the Surveyors' Association of West Jersey held at May's Landing in mid-August 1900.[43]

As 1900 drew to a close, General Wright, now in his seventieth year, could look back on many contributions that he and his siblings had made in both Atlantic and Burlington counties. Three of his brothers: Calvin (1816 – 1879), who had served as Atlantic County's first Superintendent of Schools under the "New Jersey Free School Law"; George (1824 – 1899), who had served as Joseph Wharton's Superintendent of Property at Batsto; and Willard (1832 – 1895), who had been a physician and drug store owner in Atlantic City and who had served four terms as the city's mayor. Two of his nieces, daughters of his sister Henrietta and her husband, Lucius Henry Ingalls, had, by marriage, also made significant contributions. Niece Mary Ellen was wife of Alonzo Norton, a farmer, who became Wharton's property manager. Niece Emma was the wife of Frank Middleton, who was a civil engineer and surveying partner of the

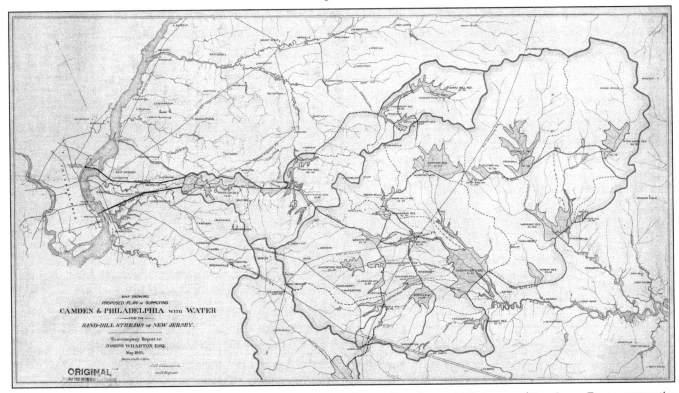

Map showing proposed plan of supplying Camden and Philadelphia with water from the sand-hill streams of New Jersey. To accompany the report to Joseph Wharton, May 1891. *Courtesy of New Jersey State Archives; Department of State.*

General's. The General's sister, Mary Ann, and her husband, William Ham, had moved to Elwood in 1864, where they established a farm. Sister Ellen's collaboration with the General gave their descendants the initial manuscript, *One Line of the Wright Family,* that makes tracing the history of this remarkable family possible.

On December 28, 1900, the General was stricken with paralysis.[44] Six days later, on January 2, 1901, the *Daily Evening Union* reported that General Wright "Passed Peacefully Away at Noon Today."[45] The cause of his death, as recorded in the "State of New Jersey Report of Death," was a cerebral hemorrhage. Now the laborious task of settling his estate began; however, true to form, his will, dated September 6, 1899, clearly spelled out how this should be done, designating "the Camden Safe Deposit and Trust Company of Camden City, New Jersey, a corporation under the laws of said State," as executor.[46]

The General's high regard for Frank Middleton, "the husband of my niece Emma Middleton," is apparent in the will. He indicates that if Frank is still in the business of surveying and engineering at the time of his (Wright's) death, he is to receive "all the instruments belonging to me, and by me used at surveying and engineering; all the implements by me used for making maps, etc.; all field notes of surveying in the office used by me; and all text and hand books belonging to me, that were used by me, pertaining to or used at surveying and engineering."[47]

The General's obvious love of learning and appreciation of Frank is revealed further on in the will when it is written: "My books called the *Encyclopedia Britannica,* consisting of thirty or more volumes, I give to the said Middleton, also the ten volumes of *Stoddards Lectures* and the volumes of books by Spofford late Librarian at Washington D.C."

John S. Risley, Surrogate of Atlantic County, appointed Frank Middleton, along with "two disinterested freeholders," to make a "true and perfect inventory and appraisement of the personal property of Elias Wright deceased." The General's three-story home, referred to as a "Cottage" situated at 24 North Pennsylvania Avenue in Atlantic City, remains standing in 2017. Now divided into rental apartments, it is undoubtedly far less imposing than it must have been at the beginning of the twentieth century, when it was filled with a treasure trove of Wright family furnishings, including multiple bedroom sets, a piano, statuary, marble top tables, many tables and chairs, a silver service, table china, cooking utensils, and even two cases of stuffed birds.

Joseph Wharton's tribute to the General, dated May 28, 1901, reflects the friendship and great respect that developed between the two men during their quarter century of working together. It reads, in part, "The world in which he lived is better for his work and for his example. Two Bible promises apply to him: 'Seest thou a

24 North Pennsylvania Avenue, side view on a rainy July morning 2015. *From the author's collection.*

man diligent in his calling; he shall stand before princes, he shall not stand before mean men.' And 'Well done good and faithful servant: enter thou into the joy of the Lord.'"[48]

John Hall added to this praise when he wrote that during his tenure as Wharton's surveyor and land agent, Elias Wright surveyed over 100,000 acres of land, some of which had titles dating back to 1720 and included several owners and many conditions. "It is an enduring monument to his industry and energy and also to the tenacity of purpose of Joseph Wharton, who has saved much trouble for his successors by clearing up titles and boundary lines in Southern New Jersey."[49]

ENDNOTES

Betsy Carpenter "met" Brevet Brigadier General Elias Wright while serving as a docent at the Batsto Mansion in Wharton State Forest. The docent script noted that Wright was once Joseph Wharton's land agent and surveyor. Her challenge was to discover exactly who this Civil War veteran was. A long-time resident of Chatsworth before moving to Mount Laurel in 2014, Carpenter applied her research skills and love of the Pines in a search that took her to Durham, NY; Carlisle, PA; Swarthmore, PA; Port Republic, NJ; and several historical societies and county administration offices. Although a graduate of Denison University and The Pennsylvania State University, she attributes her understanding of and appreciation for New Jersey's Pinelands to Stockton University where she received her B.A. Degree in Environmental Studies. Before retirement, she was employed by the New Jersey Department of Agriculture as well as the New Jersey Pinelands Commission.

1 "General Wright Dead, Passed Peacefully Away at Noon Today," *Daily Evening Union* [Atlantic City], January 2, 1901, 1; "The Late General Wright, A Serious Man and Useful Citizen Gained a Fortune," *Daily Evening Union* [Atlantic City], January 3, 1901, 1; and "General Wright Buried, Comrades of Joe Hooker Post Escorted Body to Grave," *Daily Evening Union* [Atlantic City], January 7, 1901, 1.

2 Morgan Friedman, "The Inflation Calculator," *Morgan Friedman's Homepage*, accessed March 8, 2017, http://www.westegg.com.

3 "General Elias Wright Dead at Atlantic City," *The Philadelphia Inquirer* [Philadelphia, PA], January 3, 1901, 4.

4 Mary Isabel Gibson Cone, ed., *One Line of the Wright Family*, undated document catalog #P-220Wri, Atlantic County Historical Society, Somers Point, New Jersey.

5 Ibid, 10 & 11.

6 Ibid, 17.

7 Ibid.

8 Ibid.

9 Ibid.

10 Ibid.

11 Harriet S. Sander, *The Sketches of Old Port Republic* (Port Republic Tercentenary Year, 1964), unpaginated.

12 Seymour Williams, Fellow of the American Institute of Architects, "The Franklin Inn (and Store), Port Republic, Atlantic County, New Jersey," *The Historic American Building Survey* (Library of Congress, Washington, D.C., 22 August 1940), 1-4.

13 Cone, *One Line of the Wright Family*, 17.

14 Beverly Radez, Town Historian, "A Brief History of the Town of Summit," *Schoharie County NY GenWeb site*, accessed January 12, 1997, http://www.rootsweb.ancestry.com/~nyschoha/summit.html.

15 Williams, The Franklin Inn (and Store), 3. Despite his best efforts, Benjamin is incorrect. "Gravely (Gravelly) Run" is a tributary to Great Egg Harbor River. At one time, however, Port Republic had a "Gravelly Landing" associated with its locale.

16 Friedman, "The Inflation Calculator," http://www.westegg.com.

17 William S. Stryker, *Record of Officers and Men of New Jersey in the Civil War, 1861-1865* (Trenton, NJ: John L. Murphy, Steam Book & Job Printer, 1876), 210.

18 Cone, *One Line of the Wright Family*, 18.

19 Stryker, *Record of Officers and Men of New Jersey in the Civil War*, 184 and 1496.

20 John Hall, *The Daily Union History of Atlantic City and County, New Jersey* (Atlantic City, NJ: The Daily Union Printing Company, 1899), 513.

21 Military Service Records for Elias Wright. Letter May 31, 1865.

22 Military Service Records for Elias Wright. Note from

Third Division Tenth Army Corps Headquarters dated June 3, 1865, and Special Order Number 312 dated June 17, 1865.

23 Robert F. Johnson, *Weymouth New Jersey, A History of the Furnace, Forge and Paper Mills* (Kearney, NE: Morris Publishing, 2001), 53.

24 "G. A. R. – New Post Organized," *The New Republic*, September 26, 1868, 6; "A Visit to Atlantic County – What I Saw There – Elwood, Atlantic Co., N.J.," *The New Republic*, October 16, 1869, 4.

25 Friedman, "The Inflation Calculator."

26 Johnson, *Weymouth New Jersey*, 61.

27 "Laurel Hill Cemetery, William Ham, Jan. 6, 1822 – June 16, 1876," *Find A Grave*, accessed March 1, 2017, http://www.findagrave.com.

28 Deed Book 64, pages 124 and 125, Atlantic County Clerk's Office, Mays Landing, New Jersey; dated December 13, 1876, by Mary A. Ham, Executrix of the estate of William Ham, and by Elias Wright to the Laurel Hill Cemetery Association of Elwood.

29 "An Important Experiment," *The News Journal* [Wilmington, DE], November 19, 1877, 4.

30 *The News Journal* [Wilmington, DE], November 19, 1877, 4.

31 "Proposals to Purchase Sugar Beets," Friends Historical Library, Swarthmore College, Pennsylvania, Joseph Wharton Papers (found in Wharton Papers, Record Group 5/162, Series 6 Business Papers, Box 42, Miscellaneous Notes & Documents, 1878-1909).

32 W. Ross Yates, *Joseph Wharton, Quaker Industrial Pioneer* (Bethlehem, PA: Lehigh University Press, 1987), 243.

33 Andro Linklater, *Measuring America* (New York: Walker & Company, 2002), 75, 76.

34 Robert Alexander and Lucille Alexander, compilers, *The Wrights of Wright Street—Stories of 1400 Descendants of James Wright, 1701*, vol. 2 (East Durham, NY: under auspices of Durham Center Museum, Inc., 1987).

35 "Atlantic City's Board-Walk," *The Times* [Philadelphia, PA], January 1, 1890, 2.

36 "A Suspended Company Resumes Work," *The Philadelphia Inquirer* [Philadelphia, PA], July 25, 1890, 6.

37 "Jersey News of All Sorts," *The Philadelphia Inquirer*, [Philadelphia, PA] December 7, 1891, 3.

38 "For Good Roads, A Convention of Citizens at the State House," *Trenton Evening Times* [Trenton, NJ], January 4, 1892, 1.

39 Deed Book 198, pages 234, 235, and 236, Atlantic County Clerk's Office. Friedman, "The Inflation Calculator."

40 Deed Book 234 on pages 255, 256, and 257, Atlantic County Clerk's Office. Friedman, "The Inflation Calculator."

41 "Philadelphia's Typhoid Epidemic," *The Daily Union* [Atlantic City], January 21, 1898, 2.

42 "Water from Jersey—Plan to Acquire Thousands of Acres of Pine Lands as a Source—Canal to the Delaware," *The Philadelphia Inquirer* [Philadelphia, PA], February 9, 1899, 3.

43 "Elias Wright of Atlantic City," *Bridgeton Evening News* [Bridgeton, NJ], August 17, 1890, 4.

44 Alexander, *The Wrights of Wright Street, Stories of 1400 Descendants of James Wright*, 1701, vol. 2.

45 "General Wright Dead," *The Daily Evening Union* [Atlantic City], January 2, 1901, 1.

46 Elias Wright—Last Will and Testament (Atlantic County Surrogate's Office, May's Landing, NJ), September 6, 1899, #2300, 233-241.

47 Elias Wright—Last Will and Testament (Atlantic County Surrogate's Office, May's Landing, NJ), September 6, 1899, #2300, 234.

48 Joseph Wharton's tribute to the General dated May 28, 1901, from Cone, *One Line of the Wright Family*, 19.

49 Hall, *The Daily Union History of Atlantic City and County, New Jersey*, 513.

Wright Monument in Greenwood Cemetery, Pleasantville, New Jersey. *From the author's collection.*

Elias Wright's signature. *From the New Jersey State Archives.*

Mapping the Mullica Valley:
Natural History Landscapes

Kenneth W. Able

O ur ability to understand change, including that which occurs within physical landscapes, is based on our knowledge of certain baseline conditions. This is one of the major reasons we map and compare the same landscapes over different periods of time. The distribution of animal and plant life embedded within all landscapes offers an additional rationale for measurement and study. Changes to the underwater and terrestrial portions of the landscape, along with the semi-terrestrial (areas flooded by daily tides) need to be recorded and studied; these three seeming separate landscape features are often intertwined. Where this is not obvious, it is likely that we have not examined the area carefully enough.

The Mullica Valley and its estuarine waters is a unique, relatively unaltered system, offering an inimitable opportunity as a comparative for more altered systems.[1] Furthermore, in today's world, and that of the past couple of centuries, we cannot reasonably understand this part of the landscape and its natural history without including human modifications as a substantial part of the landscape.[2] All of these notions are part of the rationale for my interest, and they provide the basis for a full-length study, currently in preparation, on the natural history of the Mullica Valley, with a special concentration on the underwater landscape.

The landscape-level importance of the Mullica Valley proves most evident when we overlay the boundaries of the valley on to that of the Pinelands Natural Reserve and other federal and state holdings (Fig. 1). The Pinelands, which cover much of southern New Jersey, surround and protect the majority of the Mullica Valley and the upper portion of the watershed. Both of these, and more specifically the Mullica Valley, enjoy some of the lowest human population densities

in the state. The lower portion of the watershed has an even lower population density, due to its wetland and riverine setting. This low population density is evident, regardless of whether you view the watershed from

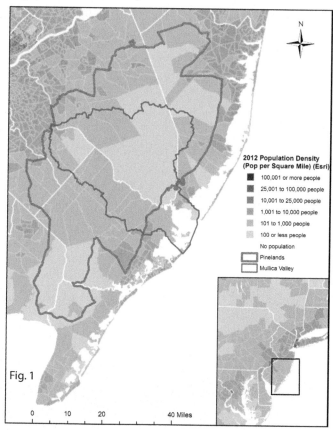

Fig. 1. Human population density measured within the New Jersey Pinelands, the Mullica River – Great Bay watershed, and the surrounding areas using ArcMap software (ESRI). The 1994 edition of the Pinelands boundary is from the New Jersey Department of Environmental Protection (NJDEP), the Office of Information Resources Management (OIRM), and the Bureau of Geographic Information Systems (GIS). Watershed shape data is provided by the NJDEP and the Division of Watershed Management (DWM).

the water or from the air. A boat trip from Little Egg Inlet, upstream into the Mullica River, clearly indicates to what degree the shoreline remains undeveloped and retentive of its salt and freshwater marshes and also retains forestation in the adjacent upland. This becomes even clearer the farther upriver you travel into the surrounding watershed. In the bay and the upper watershed, with the exception of the Mystic Islands, only the small communities of Lower Bank, Green Bank, and Sweetwater disturb the natural shoreline, which is largely dominated by Wharton State Forest.

From an aerial view, the low levels of human occupation grow more and more evident. On a helicopter ride during the fall of 2015, thanks to the generosity and expertise of Judy Redlawsk, a similar path up into the watershed revealed the extensive marshes of the lower valley (Fig. 2, 3). This made finding my location from the air difficult. The Rutgers University Marine Field Station (located inside of Little Egg Inlet), the abandoned Crab Island fish factory on Crab Island, and the end of Sooys Landing Road in Port Republic provided some landmarks as the only actual hints of human presence (Fig. 4, 5, 6). Farther upstream, the major tributaries such as the Bass River, the Wading River, and the bridge at Lower Bank in the Mullica River acted as the only visible landmarks (Fig. 7, 8). As we traveled even farther upstream into the Wading River, freshwater marshes and beds of water lilies became visible (Fig. 9). The remaining landscape comprised a green belt of

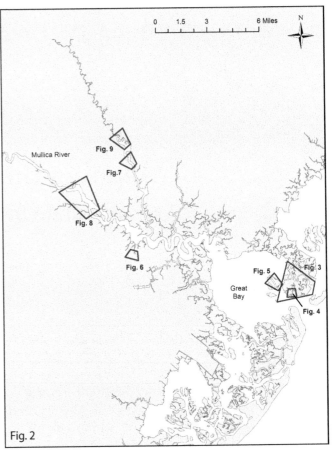

Fig. 2. Locations of aerial photographs (for the following figures) in the Mullica Valley. *Image courtesy of Kenneth W. Able.*

Fig. 3. Aerial photo of the unaltered marshes on the southern portion of the Sheepshead Meadows peninsula with the entrance to Little Sheepshead Creek, Shooting Thorofare in the foreground, and a portion of Great Bay in the background. The white buildings belong to the Rutgers University Marine Field Station, located off of Great Bay Boulevard. *Photograph courtesy of Kenneth W. Able.*

Fig. 4

Fig. 4. Aerial photo of the Rutgers University Marine Field Station (RUMFS) and the boat basin at Shooting Thorofare, with the causeway connecting it to Great Bay Boulevard. Willitts Creek runs adjacent to RUMFS and the causeway. Natural, unaltered marsh, with numerous ponds on the marsh surface, dominates the area. *Photograph courtesy of Kenneth W. Able.*

Fig. 5

Fig. 5. Aerial photo of the abandoned menhaden fish factory and water tower on Crab Island in Great Bay. Newman's Thorofare is visible in the foreground. The barely discernable linear feature, near the center of the island, is the remnant of the landing strip for the airplanes of spotter pilots, who once assisted the fishing boats to find schools of menhaden in the ocean. *Photograph courtesy of Kenneth W. Able.*

Fig. 6. Aerial photo of the extensive marshes and adjoining upland forest, which is typical along the Mullica River. Sooys Landing Road runs through the forest and out into the marshes. Manmade ditches appear in the tributaries to the creek. *Photograph courtesy of Kenneth W. Able.*

Fig. 7. Aerial photo of the bridge over the Wading River at Bridgeport, located near the upper limit of salt water intrusion. Some of the extensive marshes and upland forests, typical of the Wading River, are evident. The light green areas in the marshes are indicative of the invasive common reed, *Phragmites. Photograph courtesy of Kenneth W. Able.*

Fig. 8. Aerial photo of the bridge over the Mullica River at Lower Bank, located near the upper limit of salt water intrusion. The marsh in the lower left-hand corner of the image is the upper portion of Hog Island. The creek located immediately above it is Landing Creek. Some of the extensive marshes and adjacent upland forests are evident. *Photograph courtesy of Kenneth W. Able.*

forests that stretched to the horizon. A detailed map of land use for the Mullica Valley from 2012 further emphasizes the dominance of the landscape of forests, wetlands, and water on the landscape (Fig. 10). Some human, urban influences appear within the vicinity of Hammonton in the northwestern portion of the watershed; Indian Mills to the north and east of Hammonton; and a scattering of farms in the southern reaches of the watershed. The cranberry bogs create a distinctive signature in the landscape, scattered throughout the upper portions of the watershed, particularly in the northeast portion of the upper parts of the Wading River and the Oswego River (Fig. 10).

The waterways that fan out from Great Bay and the Mullica River, such as the Batsto, the Wading, the Oswego, and the Bass rivers, once provided the major means of transportation for privateers, early industries, bog-iron mining, and the trades of charcoal, salt hay, and timber products (Fig. 11). The writings of numerous authors deliver colorful translations of the influence these early industries had on culture and the landscape,

perhaps with folklorist Henry Charlton Beck offering the best accounts in his *Jersey Genesis*. These largely uncompromised, free-flowing rivers, bays, tributaries, groundwater, and creeks serve as the circulatory system for the watershed (Fig. 11). Some exceptions are the tributaries that have been dammed, typically to power mills and factories in times past, as at Batsto and Atsion (Fig. 12). In modern times, small dams retain water for cranberry farms.

Examining a map of the entire watershed reveals that salt marsh cordgrass dominates much of the wetlands lower in the watershed (Fig. 13). Within these wetlands, the creation of mosquito ditches represent one of the major human modifications in the lower, high salinity portions of the watershed (Fig. 14). The Civilian Conservation Corps program during the Great Depression cut many of these drainage ditches throughout the northeastern United States, including the Mullica Valley, thereby reducing breeding areas for mosquitoes. In more recent years, mosquito control methods involved another form of marsh manipulation known as Open Marsh

Fig. 9 (below). Aerial photo of the upper portion (just above what Fig. 7 depicts) of the Wading River, sometimes referred to as Half Moon Bay. In this freshwater portion of the river, the extensive forests can grow down to the water's edge. Note that there is abundant freshwater marsh vegetation (light green) in the center of the photograph. In the lower right-hand corner, extensive lily pad beds are evident. *Photograph courtesy of Kenneth W. Able.*

Fig. 10 (right). Land use/land cover within the Mullica Watershed Management Area. Agricultural wetlands indicate cranberry bogs. This 2012 data is from the NJDEP, OIRM, and the Bureau of GIS. This map was developed using New Jersey Department of Environmental Protection Geographic Information System digital data, but this secondary product has not been verified by NJDEP and is not state-authorized.

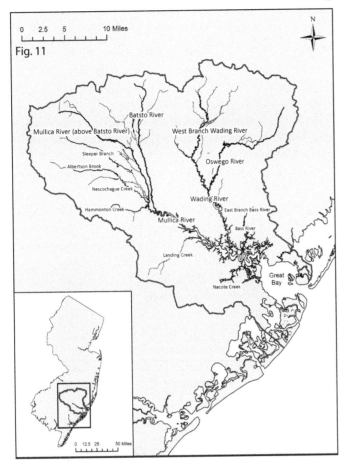

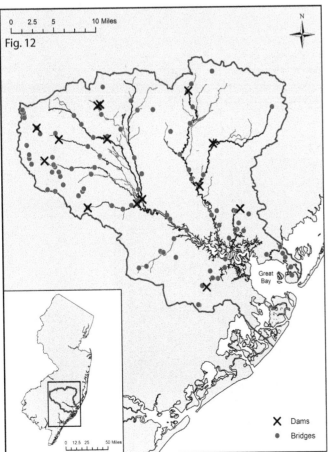

Fig. 11 (top left). Tributaries within the Mullica Valley watershed, NJ. Watershed area and 2009 coastline data provided by the NJDEP, Division of Watershed Management.

Fig. 12 (bottom left). Tributaries within the Mullica Valley watershed, with bridges and dams indicated. Watershed area and 2009 coastline data provided by the NJDEP, Division of Watershed Management. Bridge location data provided by the New Jersey Department of Transportation GIS unit.

Fig. 13 (top right). Various wetland types within the Mullica Valley watershed. The 2007 land use/land cover within the Mullica Watershed Management Area data is from the NJDEP, OIRM, and the Bureau of GIS. This map was developed using the New Jersey Department of Environmental Protection Geographic Information System digital data, but this secondary product has not been verified by NJDEP and is not state-authorized.

Water Management, an effort most evident in the Great Bay Wildlife Management Area Refuge on the shore of upper Great Bay (Fig. 14). Farther up the watershed, including the Wading River, the invasive common reed, *Phragmites*, dominate the wetlands, becoming more common over the last 100 years (Fig. 13). Even farther up into the watershed, scatters of Atlantic white cedar wetlands appear in patch-like patterns along the edges of freshwater streams (Fig. 13). They serve as a good index

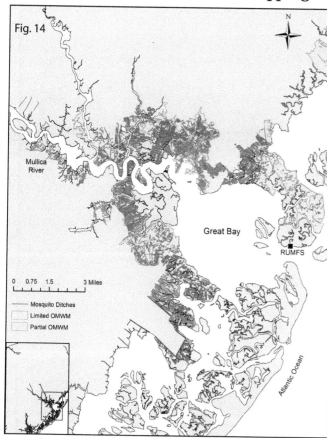

Fig. 14. Mosquito ditches and Open Marsh Water Management (OMWM) areas in the Mullica Valley watershed. Limited OMWM indicates areas with 10%-25% alteration. Partial OMWM indicates areas with 25%-75% alteration. OMWM areas and definition originated from Rachael Sacatelli (Mosquito Control Marsh Alterations in Atlantic, Cape May, Cumberland, Monmouth, Ocean, and Salem Counties New Jersey [CRSSA Draft, 2015/09/22]). OMWM areas have been modified based on ESRI aerial world imagery base map from July 2013. Mosquito ditches were digitized using an ESRI aerial word imagery base map from July 2013.

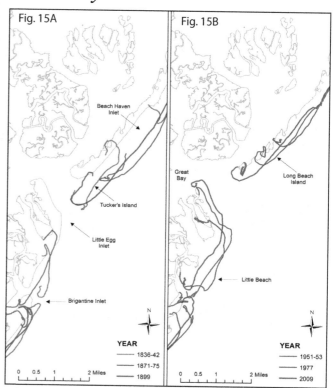

Fig. 15. Historic coastline data in the vicinity of Little Egg Inlet, NJ, for the 1800s (A) and the 1900s – 2000s (B) overlaid on the current coastline from the NJDEP, GIS unit. Coastline 2012 of New Jersey was extracted from NJDEP's Land Use 2012 data layer. Other historic coastlines provided from the NJDEP, OIRM, and the Bureau of Geographic Information and Analysis (BGIA).

of the upstream limits of salt water, because they cannot tolerate salinity.

Some of the most difficult areas to map in the valley are the portions of the barrier islands near Little Egg Inlet (Fig. 15). Over the last 150 years or so, Tucker's Island disappeared and Beach Haven Inlet shifted to the south,

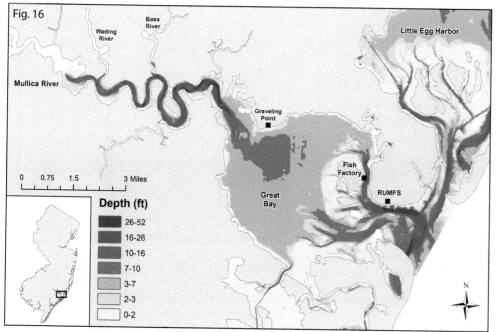

Fig. 16. Water depths, from New Jersey Inland Bays, NJ (M080) bathymetric digital elevation model (30-meter resolution), in the Mullica Valley, derived from hydrographic survey soundings collected by the National Oceanographic and Atmospheric Agency. Eighteen of the nineteen surveys used were from 1935 to 1940.

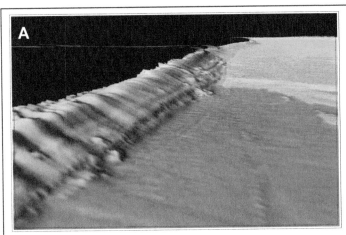

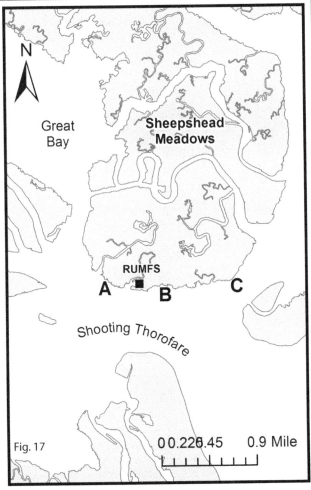

Oblique view of the eastern edge of Sheepshead Meadows showing the generally smooth slope, interrupted by scarps. These mounds may be sediment that has slumped. The scarp is about 33 ft. high. The thin red line in A and B is the entrance to the Rutgers University Marine Field Station.

Oblique view of the southern edge of Sheepshead Meadows showing numerous irregular mounds on the steep slope along the marsh edge. These mounds are slumped material from the marsh edge. The vertical extent of the slope at the edge of the marsh here is about 46 ft.

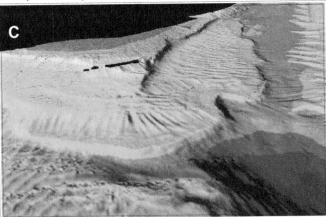

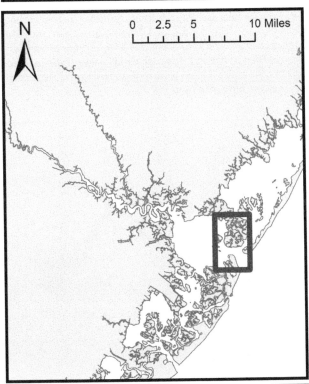

Oblique view looking north towards an underwater escarpment at the southeast corner of Sheepshead Meadows. The deepest escarpment is about 6 ft. high and goes from a depth of about 30 to 36 ft. Portions of three shallower scarps can also be seen. The depth range shown in this image is about 66 ft. and the width is about 2625 ft.

Fig. 17 (A, B, C). Underwater topography in the region where the Sheepshead Meadows meets Shooting Thorofare, near Little Egg Inlet at the entrance to Great Bay. Images generated by multibeam sea-bed mapping techniques. *Courtesy of Roger Flood and Kenneth W. Able.*

merging it with Little Egg Inlet (Fig. 15A).[3] The latter, and Brigantine Inlet farther south, are some of the last natural inlets remaining on the New Jersey shore. In recent years, Long Beach Island has been extruding to the south, while Little Beach has been extending somewhat to the North (Fig. 15B).

Beneath the water's surface, the seascape is more varied and unusual, at least in our perspective, primarily because these habitats remain largely invisible and seldom mapped. As a result, we often rely on simple tools such as nets and dredges, towed from boats on the surface, as an aid in interpreting the appearance of the bottom. In more recent years, a variety of acoustic devices (depth finders, sonar, etc.) have helped to produce more detailed maps. One dominating component of this seascape is the water depth, reaching up to 50 ft., but shallow (less than 7 ft.), or "skinny," water, dominates the estuary, particularly within Great Bay (Fig. 16). The exceptions to the shallows can be found at the lower end of the system, where deep, natural channels from Little Egg Inlet extend into Great Bay and Little Egg Harbor in southern Barnegat Bay. The depth of the the the channel extending into Great Bay reaches 40 ft. in front of the Rutgers University Marine Field Station, at Shooting Thorofare, and past the islands that, in part, comprise the flood tidal delta, including where the remains of

the old fish factory still stand (Fig. 5).[4] A deep channel appears again from the mouth of the Mullica River, up to and beyond the mouths of the Bass and the Wading rivers.

A more detailed examination completed with multibeam sonar reveals an exceptional underwater landscape. Along the southern edge of the Sheepshead Meadows, a series of steep escarpments meets the waters of Shooting Thorofare (Fig. 17). This edge, composed of sediments accumulating over thousands of years, appears to have linear features, perhaps from previous sea levels (Fig. 17A). In certain places, e.g., near the entrance to the Rutgers University Marine Field Station, numerous irregular blocks break the edge of the escarpment (Fig. 17B). At the southeast corner of the Sheepshead Meadows, where the marsh edge forms, the details of the underwater escarpment are much more visible (Fig. 17C).

A broader look at other areas in the estuary reveals much more diversity in bottom types (Fig. 18). In several places, sand waves of varying height and degrees of relief cover the bottom, primarily where there are fast currents in deep channels (Fig. 18B, 18D), a feature previously noted.[5] Farther upstream, in the vicinity of Hog Island, the varying depths throughout the main channel are obvious with the highest waves—not of sand, but of decaying plant material (Fig. 18A). An underwater

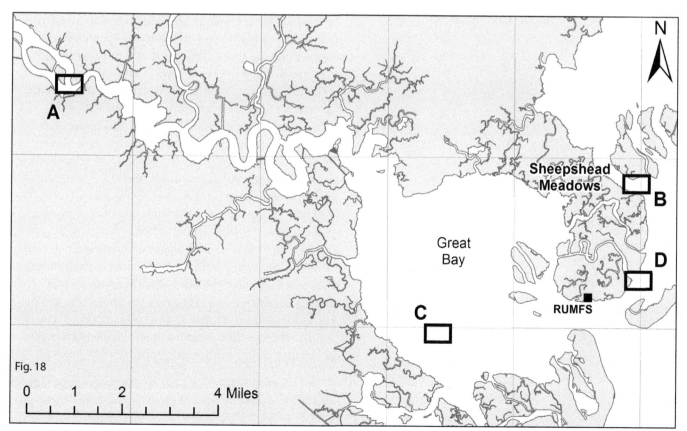

Fig. 18. Underwater topography at four sites in the Mullica Valley watershed. Images generated by multibeam sea-bed mapping techniques. For expanded views of Sites A – D see following page. *Courtesy of Roger Flood and Kenneth W. Able.*

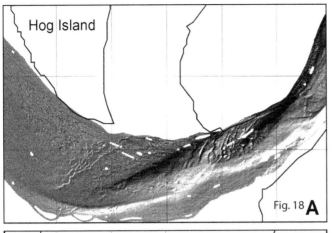

Hog Island

Fig. 18 **A**

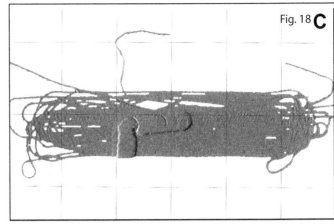

Fig. 18 **C**

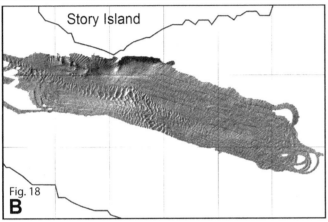

Story Island

Fig. 18

B

D Little Sheepshead Creek

Fig. 18

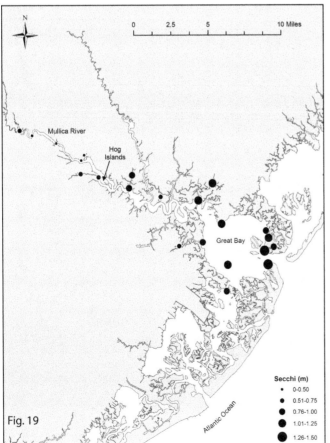

Fig. 19

camera attached to a bottom sled confirms these findings. In the same image (Fig. 18A), in the far left, small dark spots scattered across the bottom apparently stem from a drowned forest from hundreds to thousands of years ago, when a lower sea level existed. While much of the underwater landscape is undisturbed by humans, disturbance appears in the bottom sediments of the Intercoastal Waterway (Fig. 18C). In this instance, the side-to-side track of a cutter-head dredge is obvious, especially as the dredge barge changed location by rotating on its spuds on a 90-degree angle, thereby systematically removing excess sand to prevent shoaling.

Water transparency in the valley also varies along a gradient from the inlet and into Great Bay (Fig. 19). In the river, the values decline and reach the lowest level of transparency in the Hog Island area, where fresh waters from upstream meet the salt water from the ocean, causing turbidity. Along the same gradient, large green, red, and brown algaes appear most abundant in Great Bay, and then decline measurably in the lower river, and do not materialize at all in the upper river or many of

Fig. 19. Composite water transparency based on Secchi disk readings taken from samples in the Mullica Valley watershed collected by the Rutgers University Marine Field Station during July and September, 1998 – 2014. *Courtesy of Kenneth W. Able.*

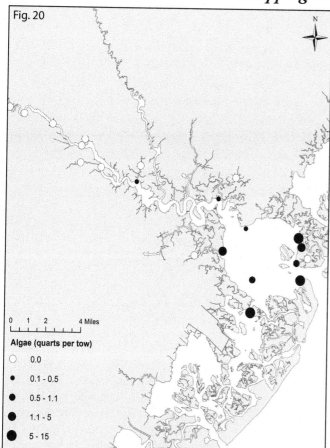

Fig. 20. Average volume of large algae in composite otter trawl samples in the Mullica Valley, as collected by the Rutgers University Marine Field Station during 2012 – 2014. The open circles indicate where vegetation was absent. *Courtesy of Kenneth W. Able.*

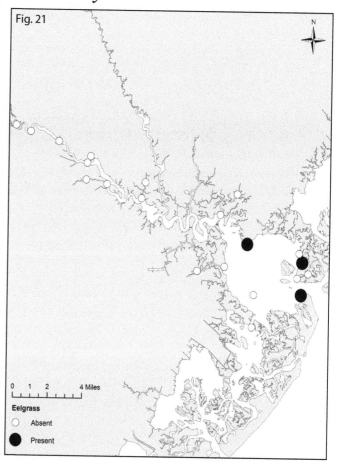

Fig. 21. Presence (closed circles) and absence (open circles) of drifting eelgrass in composite otter trawl samples during 2012 – 2014. Eelgrass values represent dead leaves apparently transported from adjacent beds within Little Egg Harbor. *Courtesy of Kenneth W. Able.*

the tributaries (Fig. 20). No eelgrass grows in the valley, but the blades are often observed floating at the surface or caught in bottom trawls in Great Bay. In late summer, when the grass blades slough off, tidal- and wind-driven currents from Little Egg Harbor carry the ribbon-like leaves into Great Bay (Fig. 21). Another vascular plant, widgeon grass, does grow in the valley, but is limited to marsh pools and lower salinity areas, such as the Bass and the Wading rivers and small tributaries upstream.

Hard clams and oysters, the dominant invertebrates (those animals without a backbone), live in the bottom-layer sediments (Fig. 22). The hard clams are commonly found throughout much of Great Bay, with the highest densities existing in the lower bay. In recent years, oysters, found in small numbers throughout the bay and lower river, represent a resurgence of this bivalve in the Mullica River. During the late nineteenth and early twentieth centuries, commercial oyster fisheries pulled

Fig. 22. Oyster and hard clam density in the lower Mullica River and Great Bay. The white areas in Great Bay and Mullica River indicate no oysters or clams found. Oyster and hard clam data from 1984 and 1988, respectively, is provided from the NJDEP, Division of Fish and Wildlife.

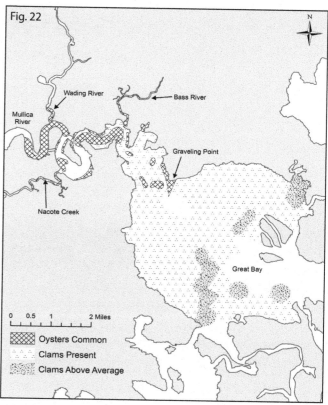

oysters by the thousands of bushels from this area in New Jersey. Today, the oysters are most abundant from Graveling Point to above the Wading River, in the main stem of the river, and in the lower portions of tributaries, such as the Bass and the Wading rivers and Nacote Creek (Fig. 22).

Ultimately, mapping the terrestrial, semi-terrestrial, and underwater habitats aids in confirming the uniqueness of the Mullica Valley watershed. In particular, the watershed provides numerous natural habitats, both above and below the water's surface, from extensive tidal salt and freshwater marshes, to abundant, undammed tributaries, and a variety of underwater depths of varying topographies in an extensive watershed with relatively few human impacts. The Mullica Valley's inclusion in the Jacques Cousteau National Estuarine Research Reserve further complements what local scientists already know about the uniqueness found here. Thus, this exceptional system provides an irreplaceable treasure, especially in the densely-populated state of New Jersey and the northeastern U.S. The valley serves as a natural laboratory for studies of sea level rise, invasive species, and other natural dilemmas facing coastal areas, as well as an exceptional venue for research, education, and gaining managerial insights.

Endnotes

Staff at the Rutgers University Marine Field Station (RUMFS), especially Ryan Larum and Christine Denisevich, assisted in the gathering of literature and preparation of maps and images. Carol Van Pelt carefully prepared several typescript drafts of this manuscript.

Ken Able is a Distinguished Professor in the Department of Marine and Coastal Sciences and is Director of the Marine Field Station at Rutgers University. His interests are diverse and include the life history and ecology of fishes with emphasis on habitat quality as well as the natural history of the Mullica Valley.

1   Michael J. Kennish, "Jacques Cousteau National Estuarine Research Reserve," *Estuarine Research, Monitoring, and Resource Protection* (Boca Raton, FL: CRC Press, 2004), 59-115.
2   Kenneth W. Able, "Natural History: an Approach Whose Time Has Come, Passed, and Needs to Be Resurrected," *ICES Journal of Marine Science: Journal du Conseil* 73,9 (2016): 2150-55. Doi:10.1093/icesjms/fsw049.
3   Gretchen F. Coyle and Deborah C. Whitcraft, *Tucker's Island* (Charleston, SC: Arcadia Publishing, 2015).
4   Kenneth W. Able, *Station 119: From Lifesaving to Marine Research* (West Creek, NJ: Down The Shore Publishing, 2015).
5   Michael J. Kennish, Scott M. Haag, Gregg P. Sakowicz, and Richard A. Tidd, "Side-Scan Sonar Imaging of Subtidal Benthic Habitats in the Mullica River – Great Bay Estuarine System**" *Journal of Coastal Research*, Special Issue 45 (2004): 227-40. doi:10.2112/si45-227.1.

Dennisville Landing. The Landing at Dennisville hosts three work-a-day vessels in this early twentieth-century view, including Augustus J. Meerwald's oyster schooner, Martha Ann, another unidentifiable schooner, and an unknown sloop with its stern towards the photographer. Based on the vessel's registration number, it appears the Martha Ann dates to the 1860s and her companion schooner at the landing looks as older or older. The timber bulkhead and cribbing along the right shore mark the former location of the B. S. Leaming Shipyard. Likewise, across Dennis Creek, J. M. Diverty operated another shipyard during the nineteenth century. The bridge behind the tied-up vessels carried a road that would become Route 47, the Delsea Drive. The New Jersey State Highway Department replaced this wooden span in 1928 with a concrete crossing. Onshore can be seen the provision store of Captain Edwards, the home of C. M. Read, and the gristmill of M. Trenchard. On this day, the landing had an elegant visitor that is somewhat oddly out of place: the sleek gasoline yacht Nepahwin has joined the working boats at Dennisville. Constructed during 1907 in Camden, New Jersey, at the yard of E. H. Godshalk & Company, Philadelphia naval architect J. W. Hussey designed this 70-foot cruiser for use up and down the Atlantic seaboard. Her draft was a mere 3.5 feet, allowing her to visit shallow waterways such as the Dennis Creek. The yacht's original owner, W. F. Harris of Newark, New Jersey, enjoyed his pleasure craft for about four years, but, by 1911, he had sold it to Senator Edwin W. Hooker of Hartford, Connecticut, and she ceased her visits to South Jersey waters for those of New York and New England.

Off Course in a Raging Sea:
Captain William M. Phillips and
the Plight of the Schooner Benjamin E. Valentine

Paul W. Schopp with Anthony Ficcaglia

Successive generations of the Estell family became prosperous landowners in southern Atlantic County, New Jersey. From the late eighteenth and into the early twentieth century, the Estells derived wealth principally through the exploitation of the natural resources found on and in their lands. The family engaged in interrelated industries such as "lumber and naval store production, boat building, ... and glassworks."[1] The history of this locally influential family should receive greater attention. Fortunately, Special Collections at Stockton University's Richard E. Bjork Library has recently received a generous donation of several hundred documents related to the Estell (later the Bourgeois) family. Known collectively as the Rebecca Estell Bourgeois Collection, the materials found within this archive includes land deeds, family letters, and materials describing the Estell Glassworks and other industrial activities along with the family's maritime interests. As these materials become better known and understood, along with related documents found in various other repositories across Atlantic County, historians will gain a better grasp of economic and social structures within the southeastern section of South Jersey.

A small file of documents found in the Estell Collection at Stockton provides a glimpse of events that, while not unusual for the time period, would cause most nineteenth-century ship owners and mariners to be more sober and vigilant. The documents describe one of Daniel Estell's trading vessels, the schooner Benjamin E. Valentine, on a routine voyage to deliver a cargo of corn meal and rye flour from Philadelphia to New York City.

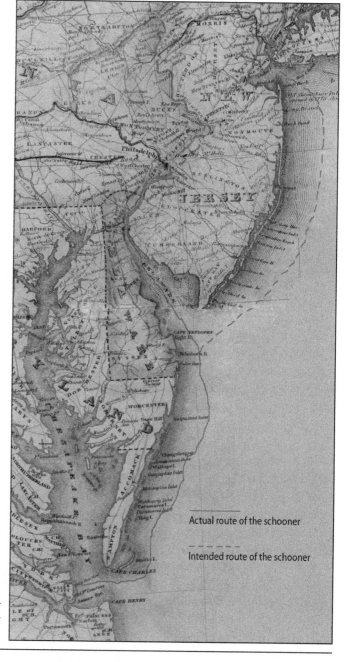

Actual route of the schooner

Intended route of the schooner

Adapted from *Map of the United States Compiled from the Latest and Most Accurate Surveys by Amos Lay, Geographer & Map Publisher, New York* (London, 1834). *Courtesy of the Library of Congress.*

What began as routine for the schooner and its captain, William M. Phillips, quickly spiraled out of control. Sailing during the heart of winter, the vessel was caught at sea in a Nor'easter gale in January 1831. The ship's perilous voyage culminated in an expensive loss of cargo, time, and necessary ship repairs. William M. Phillips, captain of the schooner, received orders from its owner, Daniel Estell Jr., to deliver his cargo of corn meal and rye flour to New York City after loading the shipment at the port of Philadelphia.

Documentation describes the schooner BENJAMIN E. VALENTINE as "of Egg Harbour," indicative of its home port and strongly suggesting that Daniel Estell Jr. had purchased the vessel from its former owners. At least one crew member, First Mate Aaron Somers, hailed from Atlantic County, further cementing the vessel to the Great Egg Harbor area. It is currently unknown where able-bodied seamen Jenkins Williams and Elhaden Burton, the crew of the schooner, called home.

ORIGINS OF THE SCHOONER

A shipyard, likely in Philadelphia, completed the schooner BENJAMIN E. VALENTINE during the first three months of 1828 as the initial mentions of her arriving in or departing from a port begin to appear in newspapers during early April 1828.[2] The schooner's namesake, Benjamin Eyre Valentine, was born in Philadelphia during May 1801 to Jacob and Elizabeth Ann Eyre Valentine, with Jacob a progeny of the New York Valentine family.[3] Benjamin carried his maternal grandfather's given name and surname. Benjamin Eyre was a master shipwright who constructed a number of privateers on the eve of the American War for Independence at his shipyard in the Kensington section of Philadelphia.[4]

Upon completing his education, Benjamin E. Valentine began his business career as a commission merchant.[5] By November 1824, however, Benjamin served as an agent for the nascent New York and Schuylkill Coal Company.[6] The firm's anthracite moved via canal barges down the Schuylkill Navigation Company's slackwater navigation system and then transhipped into schooners and other vessels at Philadelphia for the trip to Manhattan.[7] The company experienced tremendous growth in business and the need for ships to move the coal to New York became quite severe. The company initially used four brigs of about 150 tons burthen weight each, but more were needed.[8] The firm placed advertisements in both New York and Philadelphia newspapers seeking to engage ten additional coastal schooners, which the company promised to keep constantly employed moving coal and other cargo between the two port cities.[9] The coal

supplier faced an unrelenting demand for the relatively new fuel in New York, resulting in the firm contracting for the construction of its own vessels, beginning with the schooner BENJAMIN E. VALENTINE. Built as a coal schooner of about 125-ton burthen weight, the vessel was well-suited for other types of bulk cargo like corn meal and rye flour. Most schooners of this time period carried two masts with the mainmast being the taller of them. Virtually all of this type of two-masted schooner carried a gaff or fore-and-aft sailing rig, where the sails featured four-corner attachment and the top of the sail fastened to a spar known as a gaff, by which the crew could raise and lower the sail. The schooners also featured jib sails extending forward from the foremast (first mast rear of the bow) to the bowsprit and added jibboom and even a flying jibboom, providing additional speed.

While three-masted schooners began to appear at the turn of the nineteenth century, they were not common and rather a novelty. For almost the first six decades of the nineteenth century, owners and shippers alike preferred two-masted schooners for the coastal trade. The combination of their relatively low cost, speed, agility and capacity made them the perfect shipping modality. Only as wooden shipyards had the capacity to build larger schooners did the two-masted schooner end up relegated to serve as a special purpose vessel such as oystering.

THE FATEFUL VOYAGE

On January 6, 1831, Captain William Phillips ended a six-day voyage from New York City to Philadelphia, carrying a load of bulk plaster from Gotham to the Quaker City.[10] Upon discharging the cargo, Daniel Estell Jr. engaged the schooner to carry his cargo to New York City, along with whatever other commodities could be accommodated for other shippers. After the crew and the stevedores completed loading the lading, the schooner cast off from Philadelphia on January 10 at 10:00 a.m., despite the very cold morning temperatures, and embarked on sailing down the Delaware River. The ship likely departed on an ebbing tide and Captain Phillips used the winds then coming out of the northeast to propel him downriver, but progress was slow. Phillips and his crew did not reach the open ocean until January 13, probably due to the ever thickening river ice.

Despite all attempts by the crew to take the schooner up along the New Jersey coast to New York Harbor, Phillips reported that Cape May stood eleven miles north of the schooner's position at 2:00 p.m. on the 13th. The gale-force winds of the Nor'easter drove the BENJAMIN E. VALENTINE farther and farther down the Atlantic coast and away from the intended destination of Manhattan. The captain and his crew continuously battled the storm-generated winds and waves throughout the next few days, making and taking in the sails, battening down the hatches, and futilely attempting to turn northward.

In an account reminiscent of the song "Wreck of the Edmund Fitzgerald,"[11] at 8:00 a.m. on January 15, the winds increased and carried away the jib, jibboom, and bowsprit, along with other sails. Three hours later, the schooner lost part of its deck cargo and the jolly boat (a small skiff) hanging from davits off the stern. The starboard bower anchor broke loose and dropped from the bow into the raging ocean, causing a drag and imperiling the ship in the midst of the storm. Captain Phillips ordered the crew to cut the rope attached to the anchor to preserve the vessel. While engaged in cutting the anchor rope at the bow, the rudder head at the schooner's stern split and the body of the rudder sprung in its brackets while breaking one of the upper rudder irons, which attached the rudder to the vessel, making navigation far more difficult. Following these several calamities, the crew set about to make what repairs they could, given the severity of the weather.

The following day, the sustained winds blew at gale force and beyond and, at 10:00 a.m., the BENJAMIN E. VALENTINE lost its top gaff sail. During the ensuing nine days, the crew and the schooner escaped destruction numerous times and continued in their attempts to make repairs to the sails and rudder while constantly adjusting the sail array to meet the wind conditions. The captain often heaved to, meaning he brought the schooner to a stop in a position across the wind, risking being swamped by the crashing waves. At 2:30 p.m. on the 24th, the crew sounded the water depth and found it to be seven fathoms of water and the captain ordered the vessel again to heave to. At that point, Phillips scanned the shoreline and found the schooner was off Hog Island, located along the lower eastern shore of Virginia. He consulted the crew and all hands recommended they proceed to the nearest port for repairs, rather than making any further attempt to reach their original port of destination, New York City. The vessel and its rigging was completely clogged with ice, making any sail adjustments quite laborious.

At 9:00 a.m. on the 25th, Captain Phillips plotted a course for Norfolk while passing Smith Island, Virginia. At noon, the vessel anchored at the Horse Shoe Shoal, located near Old Point Comfort, Virginia, while the winds shifted and began coming out of the southwest, warming the temperature. The following day, the BENJAMIN E. VALENTINE got underway at 5:00 a.m. and finally arrived in Norfolk Harbor at 11:00 p.m., ending fifteen days of terror, determination and exhaustion.

SURVEYING THE DAMAGE

On January 27, Captain Phillips and his crew sought out a public notary in Norfolk to make a deposition of what had occurred during their harrowing voyage on the BENJAMIN E. VALENTINE. Based on the partially printed form that Virginia Public Notary Henry H. Dentzel used in taking the deposition, it was a routine method that officers and crews of distressed vessels used to account for any damage and loss due to storms. The preceding account of the voyage during the Nor'easter was derived in large measure from the deposition that Dentzel prepared.[12]

On the same day, customs officer Jacob Vickery and two assistants, Isaac Talbot and a B. English, arrived to inspect the woeful schooner at the invitation of Captain Phillips. The inspectors reported the vessel's cargo included meal and rye flour and then confirmed the damage to the rudder as well as finding the waist boards on the schooner partially damaged, along with the upper works and deck drains. The men found the jolly boat and the starboard bower anchor missing and the mainsail somewhat injured while the gaff foresail, flying jib and boom with all attendant blocks, handling and stayed lines were gone with the sails. The inspectors observed that the vessel had been "knocked down on her beam a starboard at sea" causing probable damage to her ground gear. The men sum up their written report with the following statement:

> Taking into consideration, the apparent distressed condition of the Saw Schr. We do hereby recommend that her deck Load be discharged for an examination. & that so much of her Cargo be unladen as to ascertain the condition of the ground tier of the same. That her upperworks be caulked, and that she be furnished with a new Rudder, Ruddercase, Anchor, Jolly boat & falls, Gaff Forsail, flying Jib & boom, Whipp, & what standing and running Rigging & blocks, that may be required to fit the same, that her waistboards & mainsail be repaired, and that she be furnished with all such of the necessaries that may be required to put her in a seaworthy condition to proceed on her destined Voyage.

> Given under our hands Norfolk
> January 27th, 1831

> | Jacob Vickery | (seal) |
> |---|---|
> | Isaac Talbot | (seal) |
> | B. English | (seal)[13] |

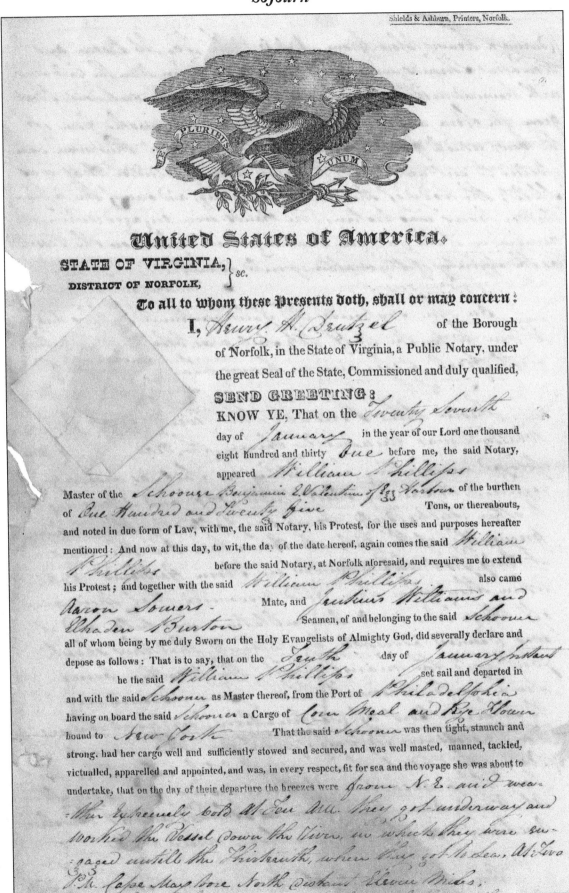

Shields & Ashburn, Printers, Norfolk.

United States of America.

STATE OF VIRGINIA, } *sc.*
DISTRICT OF NORFOLK,

To all to whom these Presents doth, shall or may concern:

I, *Henry H. Drutzel* of the Borough of Norfolk, in the State of Virginia, a Public Notary, under the great Seal of the State, Commissioned and duly qualified,

SEND GREETING:

KNOW YE, That on the *Twenty Seventh* day of *January* in the year of our Lord one thousand eight hundred and thirty *One* before me, the said Notary, appeared *William Phillips* Master of the *Schooner Benjamin E Valentine of Egg Harbour* of the burthen of *One Hundred and Twenty five* Tons, or thereabouts, and noted in due form of Law, with me, the said Notary, his Protest, for the uses and purposes hereafter mentioned: And now at this day, to wit, the day of the date hereof, again comes the said *William Phillips* before the said Notary, at Norfolk aforesaid, and requires me to extend his Protest; and together with the said *William Phillips* also came *Aaron Somers* Mate, and *Jenkins Williams and Elhaden Burton* Seamen, of and belonging to the said *Schooner* all of whom being by me duly Sworn on the Holy Evangelists of Almighty God, did severally declare and depose as follows: That is to say, that on the *Tenth* day of *January Instant* he the said *William Phillips* set sail and departed in and with the said *Schooner* as Master thereof, from the Port of *Philadelphia* having on board the said *Schooner* a Cargo of *Corn Meal and Rye Flour* bound to *New York* That the said *Schooner* was then tight, staunch and strong, had her cargo well and sufficiently stowed and secured, and was well masted, manned, tackled, victualled, apparelled and appointed, and was, in every respect, fit for sea and the voyage she was about to undertake, that on the day of their departure the breezes were *from N. E. and wea= ther Extremely cold At Ten AM they got underway and worked the Vessel down the river in which they were en= gaged untill the Thirteenth, when they got to Sea, At Two PM Cape May bore North distant Eleven miles,*

First page of the deposition describing the events that led to the Benjamin E. Valentine seeking port in Norfolk, Virginia. Dated January 27, 1831. *Courtesy Special Collections and Archives, the Richard E. Bjork Library, Stockton University.*

Captain Phillips requested that the same inspectors return to the vessel for an examination of the cargo hold and its contents, along with what remained of the deck cargo. This second inspection occurred on February 1, 1831. The surveyors found the cargo properly stowed and braced, but many bags and barrels of corn meal and rye flour had suffered damage due to the excessive water that entered the stowage during the storm, "as it is apparent to us that most of the damage is on the Starboard side from the deck downward, and this being the side on which she was knocked down while at Sea."[14] The reference to "she was knocked down" here and "knocked down on her beam a starboard at sea" on page 47 refers to the starboard (or right-hand) side of the vessel being completely submerged for a short duration due to the force of the wind and the wave. This caused seawater to rush into the cargo hold and elsewhere in the vessel, flooding portions of the hull and the bilge, requiring the crew to man hand-operated deck pumps to remove the water. Upon submitting these two written assessments to Henry H. Dentzel, he signed and certified the documents and affixed his notarial seal.

Following the repairs necessary to again make the BENJAMIN E. VALENTINE seaworthy, the schooner departed from Norfolk for New York on February 18th. Captain Phillips penned a letter to Daniel Estell Jr. before the schooner cast off. He wrote:

Norfolk February the 18th, 1831

Der Ser - i now take this opertunity of Riting to you that I am now in Norfolk. I shall sail to Day for new york. I Received your letter yestuarday Rote on the 9th of February [and I was glad to her from you] and I in form you that I have got the Schooner in good order as ever she wase and to in form you when I get on to new York I am comming home and to in form you that one third of the cargo had to Bee sold and all the old rigen that was condemned and I will in form you that I never experienced such a gale of wind and cold weather in my life. I cant tel you yet what the Schooners Bills is yet and to in form you that Duncan & Robenson duze my bisens in Norfolk - - I find them to Bee ver nise and I want you to Rite to me in new york in the min care of James R. Rapley new york.

I shall consine ~~my~~ the schooner to Baldwin & Forbes Coffeey house slip new York

Ser I am yours Mr junr D. E. Estill]

William – M – Phillips[15]

Daniel Robinson, of the Duncan & Robinson shipyard where the BENJAMIN E. VALENTINE underwent repair, also wrote to Daniel Estell Jr., informing him that the schooner had sailed from Norfolk and the cost of the repairs:

Norfolk 21st, Feb 1831

Mr. D. E. Estell Jr.
Steven's Creek
Jersey

Dr Sir,

At the request of Capt Phillips I inform you that the Sch Benj. E. Valentine sailed from this port on Saturday last for New York – Her expenses amt to $907.72, all the documents have been forwarded to Mess Baldwin & Forbes who will settle the general average at NY and to whom care Capt P. requests you will write to him =

Yours Respy
Dn. Robertson[16]

Baldwin & Forbes, mentioned in the two preceding letters, was an international shipping concern established at New York City in 1818. The firm evidently handled bills of lading, insurance claims, and other issues arising for ship owners, ship crews, and shippers.

LOST TO THE WIND AND THE WAVE

The staunch schooner BENJAMIN E. VALENTINE continued sailing for the Estells, generating revenue from the cargoes she carried. The vessel's visits to New York persisted, but she also often traveled to southern ports. Merchants in Philadelphia and New York placed newspaper advertisements for selling such items as flour and tobacco, but listing that these items arrived on the schooner BENJAMIN E. VALENTINE. Despite her damage and recovery from the effects of the January 1831 Nor'easter, the schooner ran out of luck on March 29, 1834, when she again encountered a gale and went ashore eight or nine miles south of Cape Henry, Virginia. The vessel hit hard and suffered catastrophic damage to her hull, but Captain P. Hoffman and his crew survived. The cargo incurred major spoilage.[17] Declared a total loss, Lemuel and John Cornick, Commissioners of Wrecks for Princess Anne County, advertised a wreck sale to be held on the beach where the BENJAMIN E. VALENTINE went ashore (see below).[18] This sale ended the saga of the schooner.

WRECK SALE.—On Wednesday, the 9th inst. on the beach about 8 or 9 miles S. of Cape Henry, the wreck, rigging, anchors, cables, &c. of schooner Benjamin E. Valentine; also the cargo, viz: crates and hhds, earthenware, do bottles and vials, bxs looking glasses, do window glass, kegs white lead, casks oil, do indigo, bags pimento, bales cotton yarn, bxs hats, do books, bdls steel and iron, coffee in bags bxs segars, do raisins, ten in ¼ chests, bxs dry goods, hardware, scythe blades, cutting knives, frying pans, cutting box spades, hay forks, bed cords, leading lines, &c. &c.   By order of survey,
LEML. & JOHN CORNICK.
The schooner Benj. E. Valentine, Hoffman, was from Philad. bound to Wilmington, N. C.

(Left) "Wreck Sale," April 8, 1834, *The Philadelphia Inquirer.*

(Below) Letter from William M. Phillips to Daniel Estell Jr., dated February 18, 1831. *Courtesy Special Collections and Archives, the Richard E. Bjork Library, Stockton University.*

Endnotes

Paul W. Schopp is the Assistant Director of the South Jersey Culture & History Center.

Anthony F. Ficcaglia is a graduate of the Stockton University class of 2017. With his B.A. in Historical Studies, he plans to attend graduate school and pursue his passion of writing and teaching history.

1   "Estell-Bourgeois Papers," description of gift prepared by SJCHC, 2016. Copy of text in Special Collections and Archives, Richard E. Bjork Library, Stockton University. South Jersey Culture and History Center, 2016.

2   "Marine Journal," *New York American* [New York, NY], microform edition, April 9, 1828, 3.

3   Thomas Weston Valentine, *The Valentines in America, 1644 – 1874* (New York: Clark & Maynard, 1874), 32-33.

4   Edgar Stanton Maclay, *A History of American Privateers* (New York: D. Appleton and Company, 1899), 75.

5   "Notice," *Poulson's American Daily Advertiser* [Philadelphia, PA], January 30, 1824, 3.

6   "Inland Navigation," *Poulson's American Daily Advertiser* [Philadelphia, PA], November 17, 1824, 3.

7   Ibid.

8   "Mount Carbon," *The Statesman* [New York, NY], June 17, 1825, 2; "Freight for Philadelphia," *Commercial Advertiser* [New York, NY], July 25, 1825, 1.

9   "To Coasters," *National Advocate* [New York, NY], May 25, 1825, 3.

10 "Marine List," *Philadelphia Price Current and Commercial Advertiser* [Philadelphia, PA], January 12, 1831, 1; "Marine Journal," *New York American* [New York, NY], microform edition, January 6, 1831, 2.

11 Gordon Lightfoot, "Wreck of the Edmund Fitzgerald" (Recorded December 1975; Released, 1976).

12 Henry H. Dentzel, Public Notary document for recording the accounts of distressed ships, manuscript, Rebecca Estell Bourgeois Collection, Special Collections and Archives, Richard E. Bjork Library, Stockton University, Galloway, New Jersey.

13 Jacob Vickery, Isaac Talbot, and B. English, ship inspection report, manuscript, Rebecca Estell Bourgeois Collection, Special Collections and Archives, Richard E. Bjork Library, Stockton University, Galloway, New Jersey.

14 Jacob Vickery, Isaac Talbot, and B. English, cargo inspection report, manuscript, Rebecca Estell Bourgeois Collection, Special Collections and Archives, Richard E. Bjork Library, Stockton University, Galloway, New Jersey.

15 William M. Phillips, A.L.S., to Daniel Estell Jr., manuscript, Rebecca Estell Bourgeois Collection, Special Collections and Archives, Richard E. Bjork Library, Stockton University, Galloway, New Jersey.

16 Daniel Robinson, A.L.S., to Daniel Estell Jr., manuscript, Rebecca Estell Bourgeois Collection, Special Collections and Archives, Richard E. Bjork Library, Stockton University, Galloway, New Jersey.

17 "Shipwreck," *The Philadelphia Inquirer* [Philadelphia, PA], April 9, 1834, 2.

18 "Wreck Sale," *The Philadelphia Inquirer* [Philadelphia, PA], April 8, 1834, 2.

Artensis Ashore. Caught in a late Nor'easter, on June 8, 1916, the 266-foot-long, three-masted, iron-hulled transport ship Artensis ran ashore in thick fog on the Seaside Park beach. Upon grounding hard on the sand ledge, Captain Hans Sodahl and his 19 crewmen, clinging to the rigging, sent up distress rockets. Coast Guard lifesaving crews arrived from the Toms River, Mantoloking, Chadwick and Island Beach stations. After making several failed attempts to reach the crew in a lifeboat, the guardsmen set up a breeches buoy on the beach and fired a line to the ship. The crew lashed the hawser to a mast and one-by-one, the crew reached the safety of the beach, passing 200 yards above and through the roiling breakers. It took 10 days for Merritt & Chapman Wrecking Company to pull the Artensis off the beach and back into open water to resume her voyage. Her luck ran out on July 19, 1917, when Captain Rudolf Schneider and his crew of the German submarine U-87, scuttled the Artensis while on a trip in ballast between Glasgow and Hampton Roads. She lies on the bottom off the Scottish coast.

Specialized Local Histories

Bungalow Life in the Jersey Pines: Letters of Fred Noyes Senior, collected by Judy Courter

Bungalow Life in the Jersey Pines is a collection of letters written during the spring of 1933 by Fred Noyes Sr. to his niece. These colorful letters quite literally illustrate life in the Jersey Pines. They provide a window into the life of Fred Noyes Sr., mayor of Lower Bank and father

Herbert Payne: Last of the Old-Time Charcoal Makers and His Coaling Process by Ted Gordon

A master of adaptation, Payne successfully combined the best points of the chimney-type pit and the arch-type pit, the two prevailing methods that were used throughout the Pines of New Jersey. Ted Gordon, long-time botanist and historian of the New Jersey

of Fred Noyes Jr., founder, with his wife, Ethel, of the Towne of Historic Smithville, New Jersey.
24 pages, pamphlet bound
ISBN:978-0-9976699-6-1
$5.00

Pine Barrens, describes the process in complete detail. Originally published in 1982, this 12-page pamphlet has been edited and republished with Ted's full-color images.

12 pages, pamphlet bound
ISBN 978-0-9888731-3-1
$5.00

The Outfit by Budd Wilson

Originally written in news-item format for family members, these pages introduce New Jersey State Trooper C. I. "Budd" Wilson, who served in the Outfit from 1922 – 1926. His first duty post was in rural Chatsworth, New Jersey; his first conveyance, a horse. Details of Trooper Wilson's service exemplify the New Jersey Trooper's motto: Honor, Duty, Fidelity.
24 pages, pamphlet bound
ISBN: 978-0-9976699-3-0
$5.00

SJCHC publishes specialized local histories of interest to South Jersey communities. These unusual publications provide brief points of contact between today's citizens and past community members.

"Haul Away, Boys!"
The Annual Spring Shad Run on the Lower Delaware River

First haul on the beachfront of the Gloucester Fisheries, spring 1890. Source: *Harpers Weekly*, April 19, 1890. *From the David C. Munn Collection, Special Collections and Archives, Richard E. Bjork Library, Stockton University.*

The coming of the first shad is an event the importance of which may be gastronomic or scientific according to the way you have of looking at it. . . . Gloucester, on the Delaware River, on the New Jersey side, has always been celebrated for its shad fisheries. Drift nets, and gill nets are used, and these, are sometimes from 200 to 250 fathoms [1200 to 1500 feet] in length. Deep water is a necessity for a drift net, and at the same time there must be a shelving bank, so that the nets may be readily hauled inshore. The true gill net is stretched on stakes. The illustration shows the hauling of a net, and the fishermen are putting the catch in a small boat, the shad to be at once sent to the market (see color images here and on pp. 54, 55, 56). As to value, the shad fisheries of the Delaware River are of the greatest importance. The epicure in shad is generally inclined to believe that the farther north shad is taken, the better it is. In the times of the past, however, when Philadelphia was a smaller city, and the Delaware and Schuylkill flowed unpolluted, the fish caught near that city were deemed the finest.

Quoted from *Harpers Weekly*, April 19, 1890

(above) Loading the net into the shad skiffs after the first haul has ended. Source: *Harpers Weekly*, April 19, 1890. *From the David C. Munn Collection, Special Collections and Archives, Stockton University.*

(left) Planking: the traditional way of preparing shad continues to be filleting and splitting the fish before nailing it to a wood plank. Propped near a fire, the fish is slowly roasted until done. The plank is usually cedar or sometimes oak. Devotees and gourmands often desire the shad roe to be served with the planked fish. This image shows staff from Kugler's Restaurant in Philadelphia preparing planked shad at the Mohican Club, a private social organization in Pennsauken, Camden County, New Jersey. *Courtesy of the Paul W. Schopp Collection.*

American Shad
(Clupea
sapidissima).

(above) Deploying the long drift seine from the stern of the large shad barge. Source: *Harpers Weekly*, April 19, 1890. *From the David C. Munn Collection, Special Collections and Archives, Stockton University.*

(left) Fishery account book and loose receipts from the Dwyer family for the fishery in Burlington and also at Badger's Island, across the Delaware River from Burlington on present-day Maple Beach, Bristol, PA. *Courtesy of the Paul W. Schopp Collection.*

The Weekly Times, Trenton, N.J.

May 21, 1891

The Shad Fisheries.

Those persons who enjoy the fresh shad taken from the Delaware, and who do not live closest to the fisheries have very little idea of the fishing industry to be found along its banks on either side.

At most of the fisheries the shad are sold in pairs: a large one and a small one together, unless all happen to be large and then the customer gets the advantage. Eighty cents is the customary price but the dealers get a quantity at reduced rates.

The average mesh is about five inches, although they can use as small as a three-mesh. It requires considerable care and watchfulness to properly run a fishery. Seines are very often torn and sometimes badly by a very small snag that the haul line may foul, but unless there is a big tear the mending is done after each haul, and on Sundays the seines get a general overhauling. This is like railroad work, considered a necessity. The average length of the seines used along the river is about 350 yards, but they differ at the water varies.

At each fishery is constructed a cabin where the men sleep and take their meals. When not at work the cabin is scene of various kinds of amusements. Fishermen, generally speaking, are not all practically pious and the amusements are not such as are found at a church fair or red ribbon party.

Fishermen get a move on them when there happens to be a good run of shad; then all is activity and bustle, but not confusion. Every muscle does its work, the seine glides on and off the barge, the Yale stroke is given by the after oarsman and with a whoop and a dash the old horse is started on his usual slow and easy gait to tow them to the head of the haul.

At Badger's Island, Dwyer of Philadelphia, worked a crew of some thirty colored men, and the early morning haul was made to the music of plantation melodies, and the singing could sometimes be heard for three miles. Hucksters from Hunterdon, Bucks and Mercer counties would visit these fisheries and stay until a load could be obtained, and then start out to find sale for them.

MAKING FIRST HAUL, SHAD FISHING, WASHINGTON PARK

LOADING NETS AFTER FIRST HAUL, WASHINGTON PARK

MAKING SECOND HAUL, SHAD FISHING, WASHINGTON PARK

A series of three post cards published by Washington Park on the Delaware, a large amusement park in present-day Westville, New Jersey. These men are working the fabled Howell's Fancy Hill Fishery to provide fresh shad for the restaurants at the park and at nearby Gloucester Beach. *Courtesy of the Paul W. Schopp Collection.*

SHAD-FISHERIES, ATLANTIC COAST.

Lads from Gloucester City gather along the riverfront at the fisheries, just below the Gloucester Ferry, to watch to action and buy a fish or two for their mothers. David C. Munn, who donated his Jerseyana collection to Stockton University, recollected, as a boy, just such purchases, a quarter per fish. Individual planks for cooking the shad would often be passed from father to son by Last Will and Testament.

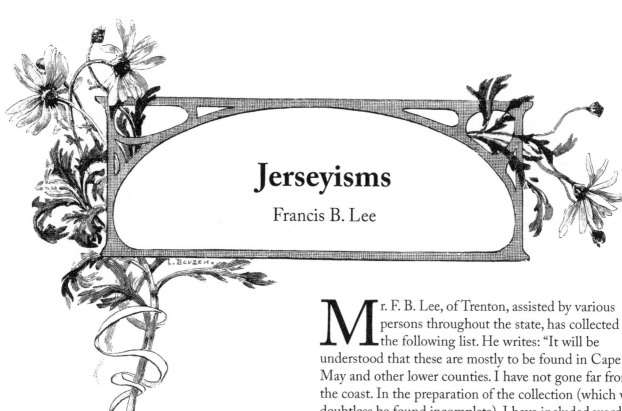

Jerseyisms

Francis B. Lee

Mr. F. B. Lee, of Trenton, assisted by various persons throughout the state, has collected the following list. He writes: "It will be understood that these are mostly to be found in Cape May and other lower counties. I have not gone far from the coast. In the preparation of the collection (which will doubtless be found incomplete), I have included words not distinctly local with those which are undoubtedly provincial. To many friends in various parts of the state I am indebted for words which appear in these pages. Those who have materially aided me are—

> Benjamin F. Lee, Trenton,
> Hannah L. Townsend, Dennisville,
> William E. Trout, Dennisville,
> Mary L. Townsend, Trenton,
> Marie Bryan Eayre, Vincentown,
> Dr. J. S. Brown, Vincentown,
> Charles G. Garrison, Merchantville,
> William Garrison, Camden."

Jersey is the form used by the natives, instead of the New Jersey of the geographies. We have followed the usage in editing the list; our abbreviations, N. J., C. J., and S. J., mean, therefore, North, Central, and South Jersey respectively. The abbreviation *q.v.* means "see the related definition."

afeared: afraid. Common in all parts of the state.

afore: common in all parts of the state. Defined in *The Century Dictionary* as *before* in place or in time: "Will you go on afore?" "If he have never drunk wine afore, it will go near to remove his fit."

age: to take one's age = to come to a birthday.

ague: An acute or violent fever. Pronounced *eigǝr*.

First published in 1896 in Dialect Notes, *the words and phrases below—Jerseyisms—provide a small and imperfect window into the language employed by nineteenth- and, perhaps, eighteenth-century citizens of New Jersey.[1] Speakers in different geographical locales developed and passed along distinctive colloquialisms. Trades and industries generated their own specialized jargons as well. A sampling of language used by the oyster, turtling, glass, and shingle-making industries is found here. So, too, are the more general idioms of day-to-day Jerseyans, especially those in South and Central Jersey. Their language is often amusing—words like "belly-wax" and "toxicatious," for example. Some display religious influence; several relate to alcohol consumption (often described quite positively); some are surprising, given modern usage—sky scraper and stepmother. Together they provide insight into a time long gone.*

alluz (ɘlɘz): common pronunciation of *always*. In Connecticut generally ɘlɘs—E. H. B.

anen, anend, anan, nan: interrogative word used to a limited extent in S. J. It implies "How? What did you say?"

anxious seat, anxious bench: the seat or bench near the altar where persons concerned for their spiritual welfare may sit during revivals. Preserved by the Baptist communities in S. J. and C. J. Fast falling out of use.

apple palsy: "plain drunk" caused by too much **jack** (*q.v.*).

aside: used in an expression "Are you aside?" meaning, "Have you your household goods in order after moving?" (C. J.)

asparagus: pronounced *spærɘgrɘs*.

ax: old form of ask. Retained in N. J. as well as in the South.

back-load: maximum quantity of game which a man can carry on his back; as, "a back-load of ducks." (Coast.)

bag o' guts: a useless individual; a "bum." (S. J. and C. J.) Also implies a big man with little brains.

barnacle: in Cape May used incorrectly for limpet found on oysters.

bateau: used only by oystermen. A small, flat-bottomed boat.

bay truck: used "along shore" for food from the bays which indent the coast; in distinction from "garden truck."

be: used for both *am* and *are*; as, "I be going," "we be going."

beant: negative form of above; used for both *am not* and *are not*.

beach: sand islands on Jersey coast. "Young" or "little beach" is new-made beach containing younger timber; "old beach," parallel ridges crowned by old timber.

beard: the byssus of mussels or the fringe on an oyster's mouth. (S. J.)

belly-wax: molasses candy. (S. J.) Often pronounced *Bailey-wax*.

belly-whistle: a drink made of molasses, vinegar, water, and nutmeg, used by harvesters at the daily nooning.

bender: common in N. J. as elsewhere. Defined in *The Century Dictionary* as "a spree or frolic," noting it as U.S. slang; it cites as Scotch slang the meaning "a hard drinker."

blatherskite: common in N. J. Defined in *The Century Dictionary* as "one who talks nonsense in a blustering way; a blusterer. A good-for-nothing fellow; a "beat."

blicky (blickie, blickey): a small bucket or pail. The variety is distinguished by an adjective, as "wooden" or "tin" blickey. Said to be Dutch in its origin, but used extensively in S. J., where there are no Dutch. In Vincentown and vicinity *blicky* is used for a coat or "juniper," such as workmen wear with overalls—a Garibaldi jacket of jean.

blister: an oyster smaller than a quarter dollar. Used from Barnegat south to Cape May.

blocks: used in North Jersey for **squares** or **streets** (*q.v.*). Demonstrating the influence of New York City, where the "block" is the regular unit of distance—20 blocks equal a mile.

bloomaries: iron forges in S. J. (Law of 1779.)

blowhard: a noisy, demonstrative, self-important person.

board-bank: floor of boards, placed on the bed of a creek near the shore, on which oysters are laid to "fatten." See **floats**.

boom-pole: pole used to hold a load of hay on a wagon. *Binding-pole* is used in this sense in Connecticut— E. H. B.

boughten: that which has been bought, as distinguished from what has been given. DeVere confines it to New York, but it is very common in N. J. *E.g.* "Were those melons boughten or guv to you?" Known in N. E., but generally used in distinction from home-made.

bounder: to scrub or wash thoroughly (the person).

boyzee: boy; as, "when I was a boyzee."

Clamming in the River. From Gustav Kobbé, *The New Jersey Coast and Pines*, Short Hills, New Jersey, 1889. All images are from this source.

brackwater: salt water of bay or river, near shore, modified by flow of fresh water. The adjective "brackish" is more commonly used.

braes: bark partially charred that slips from the wood in a charcoal pit.

brands: imperfectly burned and charred wood in a charcoal pit.

buck: a fop. Used contemptuously; "he's a pretty buck, now ain't he?" Also *buck-a-dandy*, with the same meaning.

buck-darting: a zigzag method of sailing employed on tide-water creeks.

bull: terrapin 3 or 4 inches across the belly. Five are required for a **count**, or 60 to a dozen. (S. J.)

bull nose: a useless hard clam. (Cape May County.)

bulldoze: common in Jersey. Defined in *The Century Dictionary* as "1. To punish summarily with a bull-whip; cow-hide.—2. To coerce or intimidate by violence or threats; especially, in politics, to bully; influence unfairly; applied particularly to the practices of some southern whites since the civil war."

bullrag, bullyrag: to tease, domineer over. (S. J.)

butterfingered: an adjective used to describe a person whose powers of retaining an article in his grasp are not great. (C. J. and S. J.) Known elsewhere, but generally confined to baseball.

by-and-by: pronounced *baim bai*. [Common in N. E.]

calk: pronounced *kərk*.

careful: pronounced *karfl*. [Common in N. E.]

chaw: common pronunciation for *chew*.

chinkin: boards, sticks, or clay used to fill spaces between logs in cabin building.

chunker: coal boat used on the canal. (N. J.)

cions, scions: pronounced *science* (*saiəns*) in S. J. Young growth of oak timber. Pines and cedars have no scions. To "science" (verb) is to cut off these sprouts.

clink: used of two chairs which are tilted so as partially to support each other, each having two legs on the floor.

clucker: frozen oysters. (S. J.) See **rattlers**.

cluttert: for *cluttered*. *E.g.* "cluttert into heaps."

coal: charcoal. (S. J.)

collier: charcoal-burner. (S. J.) A place in Ocean County is named "Collier's Mill."

coon oyster: small oyster attached to the sedge rather than to the usual more solid supports.

cooster: to "potter around," fuss. "What you been coosterin' at all day?" Also to caress, coddle.

count: terrapin six inches across belly, fit for market. (S. J.)

count clams: quahaugs, 800 to the barrel.

cow: six-inch female terrapin. (S. J.) One "count."

cowcumber: for cucumber.

crib: horizontal sticks piled triangularly around the **fergen** (*q.v.*) in charcoal burning. (S. J.) Sticks of cord-wood placed at right angles (usually in fours) to form a column against which cord-wood may be piled in "ranks."

crock: earthenware vessel. (Common in S. J.) Also known in N. E.

cubby: a little hollow-square cabin. (Charcoal industry.)

cubby-hole: place in a garret where refuse is stored. The word is familiar to some New Englanders in the sense of a little cozy place, behind furniture, or in a hay-mow, for instance, where one or two children might hide.

cull: to assort (oysters). Poor oysters are *cullins*.

culls: the grade next to the poorest.

cullinteens: bushel oysters; like *cullings* or *cullens*.

curricle: two-horse chaise. (Law of March 20, 1778.)

damnify: to injure. (Law of 1677, referring to hogs running loose: "in damnifying meadows by rooting.")

daubin: mud between the logs in a log house.

dicked: arrayed. Possible corruption of "decked." Not very common.

dike (*cf.* dicked): "on a dike" means showing one's finery in public.

dip: pudding-sauce.

dod (dod blasted, dod slammed, etc.): for "God" in quasi-profanity.

dominies: common in Jersey in an adjective sense. *E.g.* "a dominie-lookin' feller." Defined in *The Century Dictionary* as a schoolmaster; a pedagogue.

double up: to marry.

do-ups: preserves.

downcome: a fall or attendant disaster. Used with reference to politics.

down country: New York City and vicinity (Sussex Co.).

down felowyers: used in Cape May County to indicate people from the southern part of the county. (Corruption of *down belowyers*.)

dreg, drudge: pronunciations for *dredge* among the oystermen.

drugged: past tense of *to drag*.

dubersome: doubtful; also in form *jubersome*. (C. J.)

durgen: old horse, worn out by use. (S. J.)

Durham boat: used on Delaware River till 1835. Washington probably used them in crossing before the battle of Trenton. They were sharp-pointed, flat-bottomed scows, built to run the rapids in the hill country. They were common in the colonial period between the "Forks" at Easton and Burlington City.

Dutch cuss: term of contempt. (Metuchen.)

earnest: pronounced *ærnəst*.

errand: pronounced *erənt*. [Known also in N. E.]

extra meetins: certain periods devoted, in Baptist and Methodist circles, to special religious services of the nature of revivals.

eye opener: big drink of liquor; say, "four fingers."

fag eend: the end piece of anything.

fast land: upland near coast. (S. J.)

faze: to injure. As noun in "he went through and nary a faze." (S. J. and C. J.)

fellies: plural of *felloe*. (Law of 1766.) *Felloe* is defined in *The Century Dictionary* as "the circular rim of a wheel, into which the outer ends of the spokes are inserted; in the plural, the curved pieces of wood which, joined together by dowel-pins, form the circumference or cirular rim of a cart or carriage wheel."

fergen: centre pole in a charcoal pit, forming the central part of the **crib** (*q.v.*). (S. J.)

field: deserted farm overgrown with pine, scrub oak, and brambles. Some of these *fields*—the term is equivalent to *plantation*—are from a century to a century and a half old. Distinguishing names are Broomstick Ridge Field, Lawrence Field, etc. (Cape May County names.)

firing place: spot suitable for charcoal burning.

fist: "to make a bad fist of it"; to make mistakes or do work incorrectly.

flirch: abundant. (S. J.)

floats: (charcoal industry) irregular sods laid on "four-foot lengths," over which sand is placed. (oyster industry) pens of boards placed in fresh water, upon which oysters fatten during one tide. They are then marketable by the thousand.

folks: immediate family. Also N. E. In Connecticut I have heard men say "my folks," meaning strictly "my wife," though there were others in the family.—E. H. B.

footlin': an adjective with meaning similar to **footy.**

footy: small, insignificant. Professor Sheldon knows the word in Maine as a noun = *simpleton*. There is also a N. E. expression "footin' around" (û) = fussing, busying one's self uselessly.

funeral: "his funeral was preached" equals "his funeral sermon," etc. (S. J.)

gad: small whip used to drive cows to pasture. (S. J.) Known in N. E. in sense of *whip*.

garvey: a small scow. (Barnegat region.)

glommox, glummicks: a muss, or a conglomeration of matter. (S. J. and C. J.)

go by water: to follow the sea as a calling. (Coast.)

golly keeser: oath heard in S. J.

goodies: a fish of peculiar delicacy, much eaten on the coast. The "spot fish" of Virginia. (Atlantic and Cape May.)

goody-goody: contemptuously applied to an over-fastidious person. (S. J.)

gooseberry fool: an old-time dish of gooseberries and eggs; eaten with cream.

gorramity (*gərəmaiti*): for *God Almighty*. (S. J.)

goster: to domineer.

gosterer: one who boasts or brags.

grass: spring of the year. "I'll move out o' here next grass."

gravel also **grabble:** to steal potatoes without disturbing the hill (the act identified by the newly turned earth).

green head: a fly common in the coast district.

ground oak: to inflict injury on the person, or threaten to do so; a sort of *duress per minas*—*i.e.* duress by threats. (A ground oak is a small oak of little value.)

gulf weather: warm, moist, cloudy weather, attributed on the Jersey coast to the influence of the Gulf Stream. It is felt as far west as Trenton.

Halifax: Mr. Skillman thinks that the common enough expression, "Go to Halifax!" is a survival from Revolutionary times, and meant originally "You are a Tory; go where you belong!" This, because he has heard "Go to Nova Scotia!" in the same way (and also, "Go to Haverty-grass" (Havre-de-grace), which he cannot explain historically. Can any one account for this, or for "go to grass," which suggests a connection?).

heifers: young cow terrapins. Two or three to "counts." (S. J.)

hetchel: to tease, to call to account. Metaphor from the days of the domestic flax industry.

hether: teamster's word = *haw*; go to the left. Equivalent to **peddy whoa** (*q.v.*).

hike: of clothing, to be uneven or not to "set well."

holdfast: a sore, eating to the bone, which may come from various causes.

Sailing on Barnegat Bay.

homebringen: first coming of newly married to the house of the groom's parents, where a feast was prepared and guests were invited. "Volunteers" (uninvited but not always unwelcome guests) often came. There was music and dancing and rather free hospitality, but no drunkenness. (See **infare**, below.)

honey-fogle: to allure by traps.

horse coursers: defined as *drovers* in law of 1682.

horse-proud: adjective used of a man who has pride in his blooded stock. Similar words are used made up with names of other animals; *e.g. hog-proud.*

housen: plural of *house.*

hull: to gad about, wander, roam. "He went a-hullen all over the country."

hyper: to hurry about; to bustle at work. (Little used.)

Indian bread: fungus found underground in the pine woods. The *Tuckahoe.* (S. J.)

Infare: bridegroom's party (see **homebringen**, above). A somewhat later word than homebringen for the same festivity.

jack (apple): in Salem, Sussex, and Burlington counties, where apple whiskey is made, it is commonly called "jack." "Jersey Lightning" is hardly used by natives for this article. How widely is the word "apple whiskey" used? "Cider brandy" is the natural word to New Englanders.

jag: a small load. In S. J. a load of hay. Not used among the country people in its present slang sense. *The Century Dictionary* explains the present slang sense as a drunken condition: "to have a jag on."

jagger-wagon: light, open farm-wagon used on the roads for light work, such as carting small truck and going for the mails. (Central Burlington County.)

Jersey blue: color of uniform worn by Jersey troops in the French and Indian War.

Jimminy crickets: common in Jersey.

ketchy: changeable (weather).

kettereen: a kind of carriage. (Law of 1779.)

killick: small anchor. (Very common on coast.)

kink: used in N. J. for *kinky.* Used as noun meaning idiosyncrasy. *The Century Dictionary* defines the colloquial use of *kinky* as *crotchety; eccentric.* Also in sense of pain, "a kink in the back" = lumbago.

kip: young chicken. (Used also as call—"kip, kip.")

lap: a "hank" of thread.

lashin(g)s: plenty; abundance. "Lashins o' money."

lay-overs for meddlers: answer to prying, curious children. "What's that, ma? Do tell, won't you?" "Why, didn't I say it's lay-overs for meddlers?"

lenter: for "lean to" = an addition to a house. Pronounced *lentr, lintr,* and *lintr.*

lift the collection: take up the collection. In common use in some localities.

lobscouse: an awkward, hulking fellow.

loper: a worthless, intrusive fellow.

lug: bark. "The dog lugs at the waggin."

mam, mom, mæ: for mamma or mother.

marsh: pronounced *mæs.* [Also in N. E.]

meadow: salt marshy tract used for grazing and "shingling" (see below) in S. J.

menhaden: called "moss bunkers," "mossy bunkers," "green tails," "Sam Days," and "bony fish," in Cape May County, and "mud shad" in Cumberland County.

milchy: adjective applied to oysters "in milk"—just before or during spawning.

molasses: pronounced *merlassers, merlasses, millasses.*

mosey: to leave suddenly, generally under doubt or suspicion.

mought (maut): for *might.*

mudwallop: to soil one's self with mud. To play in the mud when fishing.

my: pronounced *mi.*

nary: never.

noggin: a wooden dipper.

noodeljees (*nûdlt sîz*): "noodles,"—thin strips of dough like macaroni, used in soup.

nothing: pronounced *nəpin*.

nubbin: imperfect ear of corn.

nutmeg: muskmelon (generic). (S. J.)

O be joyful: hilariously drunk. (Common.)

ordinary: innkeeper, in laws of Lord Proprietors. Now out of use.

ornery: common in use; extremely ordinary.

overly: used in speaking of health, etc.; *e.g.* "not overly good." Generally in negative use.

oyster grass: kelp found in oyster-beds. (Cape May.)

oyster knockers: culling tools. Double-headed hammer used to separate bunches of oysters.

pap, pop, poppy: for *papa* or *father*.

passel (for parcel): number, quantity in general. "They acted like a passel o' hogs."

patent thread: linen thread. (S. J.)

peddy whoa: teamster's word = *haw*; go to the left. Equivalent to **hether** (*q.v.*).

perfect love: an old-fashioned intoxicating drink.

periauger: oyster boat. (Law of 1719.)

petty chapman: itinerant vender. (Law of 1730.)

pick (pique?): a spite, grudge, "He's had a pick at him for months."

pile, piling, pile driver: often pronounced *spile*, etc., in N. J.

piners: those who live in the Jersey pines,—the "ridge" sections (eastern and southern) of the state.

pinxter: Whitsuntide.

pinxter-blossoms: azalea. (Albany Co.)

pit: wood stacked for charcoal burning.

platform: planked floor where oysters are freshened. (Atlantic County.) See **board-bank** and **floats.**

pool holes: holes, two to six feet deep, full of "mucky" water, found on meadows. (See Shingle Industry below.) Often *spool holes.*

pretty: pronounced *pərti, puti.*

pretty middlin' smart (*smœrt*): indicates a fair state of health. Common in N. J.

progue: pronounced *prɒg.* To search for anything imbedded in the mud, as clams, terrapins, or cedar logs, by means of a sounding rod.

quiler: holdback strap (on a horse's harness, allowing a cart to be driven backwards).

quite: not a common word in S. J. Common in C. J. in such expressions as "quite some."

rattlers: oysters in poorest condition. So called because they rattle in their shells. See **clucker.**

reach: that portion of a circuitous creek in the tide-water district between two sharp turns. Reaches are from 200 feet to a mile or more in length.

Crabbing in the Creek.

riz bread: yeast bread (not raised with soda).

rollejees (*rolitsîz*): chopped meat, stuffed in "sausage-skins" to be sliced and cooked.

salt holes: pool holes of small size filled with salt water. Frequent in marshes.

scions. See **cions.**

scoot, scoat, skeet: to leave suddenly.

scrub oak: a low-growing species, usually the first timber growth on a burned district. As soon as the larger timber grows above it, the scrub oak dies out.

set offs: sugar and cream in coffee; "trimmings."

shacklin': shiftless; lazy; going from one job to another.

shell bed: collection of oyster shells in S. J., where Indians made wampum, or dried bivalves for food.

shellers: those who open clams for market.

shenanigan: fooling or playfulness. Also expressed by "monkey business." Known in N. E.

sherk: for *shark.* Also reported from coast of Virginia.

shoots: spaces between concentric rings of oyster shells, showing years of growth.

shuck, shock: to open oysters. To husk corn.

side up: to clean up, put in order (a room).

singing sand: sand found on Long Beach, Ocean County, which emits a peculiar musical tone when the wind passes over it rapidly. It is found on a portion of beach made since 1818.

sistern: plural of *sister*. Used in Baptist and Methodist churches.

skeins: for *skene*. A dagger. (Law of 1686.)

skift: for *skiff*. A yawl used in E. J.

sky scraper: one who reaches high; one who is exalted in his own estimation.

slank: low place at side of river, bay, or cove, filled with water at freshet.

slash: swale filled with water. (Cape May.)

slews: (corruption of *sluice*) a **thoroughfare** (*q.v.*). (Coast.)

slug: a big drink of whiskey.

slummock: a dirty, untidy woman.

snag gag: to quarrel or have an irritating controversy.

snail bore: a mollusk, also called "drill," "borer," etc.

sneathe: snath of a scythe. *The Century Dictionary* defines *snath* as the curved handle of a scythe.

snew: past tense of *to snow*. (N. J.)

snoop: to pry into another's affairs; to sneak.

snub: to "canal it" on a boat; to make fast. (C. J.)

snubbin' post: post around which rope of boat is fastened in lock.

soft shells: crabs with soft shells.

souse: slangy for ears. "Bounder your souse well" means wash your ears well.

spack: pork.

spoom: to run before the wind. (Coast.)

springers: cows about to calve. (C. J.)

spung: piece of low ground at the head of a stream in the tide-water district.

squares, streets: used generally in S. J. and C. J. as unit of distance in cities, demonstrating a Philadelphia influence. Like **blocks** (*q.v.*) in N. J.

stepmother: a ragged nail or a roughness of the skin.

stick up: a long, thin oyster; so called in Cape May from the fact that it "stickups," as oystermen say, in the mud.

stirrup (n. and v.), **stirrup oil** (n.): shoemaker's term for a whipping, or punishment administered with the stirrup, or knee-strap.

stone horses: stallions. (Law of 1709.) Used in this sense in *Robinson Crusoe*.

strull: female tramp. Strulling is used of women, not in the worst, but generally in no favorable sense. "She's gone strulling to town to-day." Sometimes used of children, without regard to sex.

stuffy: close and sultry, like a **Gulf weather** day (*q.v.*).

sun down: sunset; very common.

sun up: sunrise; not common, but still in use.

swale: low land between sand ridges on the coast beaches.

sward: pronounced *sôrd*. *The Century Dictionary* defines as "the grassy surface of land, turf."

swing seat: a seat used in a wood wagon, hung from the sides. Used after unloading.

tacker: small child. The adjective *little* generally precedes the noun.

tar kiln: place where tar is tried out of pine knots.

ten fingers: oysterman's slang for *thief*. Not very common.

thawt: for thwart; rower's seat. Used to a limited extent.

thill horse: shaft horse. Not very common.

thoroughfare, throughfare (see also **slews**): long, narrow body of water connecting the bays which separate the sandy islands of the southern coast from the mainland. Reported as proper name for such passages from Maine and Virginia. In law of 1695 a "thoroughfare" was a wagon road.

three-square: a kind of grass found on S. J. meadows.

thunder-heads: cumulus clouds piled above the black mass of the storm. In Connecticut, heavy cumulus clouds which appear before a shower.—E. H. B.

tickly (tickely, ticklish) bender: running on yielding ice.

ticky: Rio coffee. (S. J. traders.)

tittavating (v = w): repairing; *e.g.* "The housens need tittavating."

tongs: oyster tongs.

toxicatious: for *intoxicating*. (Law of 1679.)

traipse: final *e* pronounced. The word has a good use in Jersey; no idea of "slackness" is attached to it, as Webster would imply. *The Century Dictionary* defines *traipes* as to gad or flaunt about idly.

truck: to barter or to trade. (Law of 1688.)

upheader: horse that holds his head high. Applied figuratively to men.

v is often prounced like *w* by the older people in S. J. A Gloucester County saying is, "Weal and winegar are good wittles to take aboard a wessel."

wain: wagon. (S. J.) Not much used.

wherries: for *ferries*. (Law of 1716.)

wind breaker: a screen or the like used to break the force of the wind.

winders: an instrument used on the oyster boats for winding the dredge line.

winklehawk: triangular tear in cloth.

The Glass Industry

Mr. William Marks, of Millville, and Mr. Charles Simmerman, chief of the State Bureau of Labor and Statistics, furnish the following list of words. Some of them are used only in the flint glass houses, others in the green glass works as well.

all aboard: used in flint glass works as order to begin and quit work.

batch: the mixture of soda and sand of which the glass is made.

bench stones: resting-place for pots inside the furnace.

blast: the ten months of the year when fire is in the furnaces.

blower: one who forms or "blows" molten glass.

blowover: bottle finished by grinding its mouth on a stone. Fruit jars are usually finished in this way.

bounty jumper: a cylindrical mould.

breast stones: sides of the furnace.

bull: glass unfit for use after the melt.

cap: top of the melting furnace.

carrier in: one who takes bottles to the annealing oven.

cordy glass: bottle glass containing strips resembling fine cords, caused by glass not being thoroughly melted, or being kept too long in pot.

cullet: waste glass.

draw pickle: wooden stick used in pot setting. (Flint glass manufacture.)

fiddle: a fulcrum for the **sheen** (*q.v.*) in pot setting.

fire out: end of the ten months' blast. Factories close during July and August.

fire over: cessation of work for the day.

flip flop: bladder of thin glass used as a toy.

flip up: an old-fashioned style of mould.

foot bench: bench around the furnace, upon which the workmen stand.

furnace: where the glass is melted in the pots.

gaffer: one who finishes bottle by putting mouth upon it.

gatherer: one who takes the glass from the pots.

get-up: one day of labor; *e.g.* "Ten get-ups (ten days) before fire out."

glory hole: small furnace where bottles are finished.

goat: two-wheeled wagon used to carry the pot to the furnace from where it is first tempered.

heel-tapped: unevenly blown (bottle).

Henry: a lie (in Millville glass houses). Perhaps the name of some notorious liar.

lamp workers: Bohemian blowers who work glass by a lamp.

lazybones: iron machine used for resting iron bars when the furnace is being cleaned or repaired.

leer: annealing oven, where glass is tempered for 24 hours.

mauer: iron plate where blower rolls his glass.

melt: process of reducing the **batch** (*q.v.*) to molten glass.

mill hands: those who make the clay stone.

monkey: small pot used in flint factories.

necktie: imperfect bottle wrinkled in the neck.

pot: the clay jar where the batch is placed during the melt. The pot is from 32 to 64 inches in diameter, and 2½ feet high; from five to ten of them go in one furnace.

pot shells: pieces of broken pots which are ground up for the making of new pots.

presser: one who presses glass in the mould.

presto: an exclamation which implies "Be careful of your language, as visitors are in the works."

puntey: iron rod with holder used to finish bottles. *Pontee* in Webster.

rack on: term used to imply the blower's loss of ware through imperfect work.

ring hole: hole in furnace where blower gets his glass for bottle work.

ring stone: stone to close the ring hole.

salt water: salts in soda which rise to surface of molten glass, and after being skimmed off, harden into cakes.

sandy glass: glass poorly melted.

shears: cutting tool used in glass making.

shear hole: hole where fire is "set."

shear to: to heat up the furnace.

shearer: the "master shearer" has charge of the furnace during the melt. His assistant is the "shearer."

sheen: long iron bar used to set pots on edge of furnace.

slocker: refuse glass.

slow fire: commence work.

snap: iron rod used to finish bottles. See **puntey.**

Port Norris.

snapper up: boy employed in glass works.

stone: clay. There is no stone in S. J., and clay takes its place.

tap: to open the **tone** (*q.v.*) of a furnace to take away refuse glass, which when it cools becomes **slocker** (*q.v.*).

tempo: a cry implying cessation of work.

tone: central space of furnace around which pots are set. The flame melting the batch circulates therein.

tube blower: one who makes tubes for lamp works. (Flint works only.)

tuck stone: stone (clay) sustaining arch over furnace grate.

yink yank: equivalent to **necktie** (*q.v.*).

The Shingle Industry

Carried on in the cedar swamps of South Jersey.

bolt: piece of cedar, 2 feet long, 6 inches wide, 2 inches thick.

break down and **windfall** are terms describing conditions in which cedar logs are found beneath the surface. The log is chipped and its condition is indicated by the odor of the chip.

butting: the process of levelling shingles.

dug ups: shingles made from logs fallen and covered with soil. Called also *mud*, *rove*, and *split*.

froe: instrument, used to **rive** (*q.v.*) cedar into bolts. A blade 16 inches long and 3 inches wide, with a handle 6 inches long at right angles to one end.

horse: contrivance for holding shingles while they are being shaved.

pool holes (*q.v.*) are caused by removing cedar logs.

progueing iron or **progue:** iron rod 4½ to 7 feet long used to **progue** (*q.v.*) for cedar logs.

rive: to cut cedar bolts into pieces ½ inches thick.

shave: to prepare rived bolts for use on roof.

shingling: the process of taking cedar logs from the meadows or swamps and converting them into shingles.

straight rift and **twisted** are two conditions (as to grain of wood) in which cedar logs are found.

tap or **cut:** a piece sawed from the log beneath the surface.

wind shakes: trees which have been twisted by the wind so that the effect is shown by the twisted grain of the wood.

Endnotes

1 The text is extracted from *Dialect Notes*, Vol. 1, 1896, pages 327-37, 382-83. This collection of *Jerseyisms* was posted on NJPineBarrens.com on September 26, 2010. You can find the electronic version here: http://jerseyman-historynowandthen.blogspot.com/2010/09/jerseyisms.html

Bibliography

Webster's Complete Dictionary of the English Language, London, 1886.

William Dwight Whitney, ed., *The Century Dictionary* (New York: The Century Co., 1889).

CHARCOALING.

Collier in Cubby.

The upper photograph depicts Buzby's Chatsworth General Store *circa* 1920; note the post office sign. The lower photograph was taken c. 1950, welcoming drivers to Buzby's. *These and all subsequent images are courtesy of the Buzby-Schmidt Collection, Special Collections and Archives, the Richard E. Bjork Library, Stockton University.*

The Rebirth of Buzby's Chatsworth General Store

R. Marilyn Schmidt

Buzby's, the Chatsworth landmark, was made famous by John McPhee in his book *The Pine Barrens* (1968). Known for its line of merchandise, Buzby's sold everything from cold cuts to shotgun shells. It was also the center of communications for the pinelands. Buzby's had served the pinelands communities since 1865 when the store was built by and initially run by the Wade family.

The Cranberry Festival is what led me to Buzby's General Store. In the 1980s Buzby's operated as a luncheonette—here the festival vendors, such as me, enjoyed breakfast—and even lunch.

Unfortunately, Buzby's closed! This was around 1988. The store remained closed for seven years and became a forlorn, neglected structure. The adjoining buildings—a garage, a barn, and an outhouse on the property—were in similar or worse condition.

At this time, my life in Barnegat Light was quiet, calm, and peaceful, interrupted only by running *Barnegat Light Press* and *Pine Barrens Press*, writing and producing new books and booklets, and selling these publications. An occasional freelance assignment completed the workday.

Wholesale accounts required traveling throughout the state. Fulfilling mail orders, in addition to selling at local festivals such as the Chatsworth Cranberry Festival, the Pinelands Short Course, and various other events, filled the days.

With Buzby's closed, the firehouse remained the only source of breakfast during the Festival. This was fine but not the same.

During subsequent years, Buzby's remained closed and continued to deteriorate. Local young people gained entrance to the store to drink and smoke and do whatever young people do. The store was a mess and locals expected it to burn.

After trying to convince friends to purchase this historic site, the response always was, "Why don't you!" Not considering the fact that I was 70 years old, living in a lovely house I had designed overlooking the Barnegat Lighthouse, I said, "Why not!"

During this time, after writing seafood cookbooks, a major seashore garden book, and before that *Harper's Handbook of Therapeutic Pharmacology* and other technical publications, I had become seriously interested in the Pine Barrens. Information I wanted was hard to find. The Pinelands Commission was an obvious source, but still I couldn't find the information I needed—where were the pines, what was in the pines—parks, forests, towns, churches, monuments, memorials, etc.? There was no one source for this information.

Slowly I began to obtain the information in bits and pieces from many places. Several years of research ended in my writing *Exploring the Pine Barrens: A Guide*. After publishing this book, a major deficiency was obvious. There was no way to identify what was in a specific area. Each item was in a separate section of the book. A map was needed to identify all the items in the book.

A phone call to a map producer, a Pennsylvania firm, enabled *Pine Barrens Press* to produce a map locating all items identified in the *Guide*. This time-consuming project resulted in a much-needed map of the Pine Barrens. And, importantly, you could determine if you were in the Pine Barrens.

An initial press run sold out quickly and the map was then reprinted in a much large quantity. Unfortunately or fortunately, both the guide and the map today are out of print (2017). Both sold extremely well and are still in demand.

Over the years, my interest in the pines and local products resulted in additional books: *The Best of Blueberries, Cranberry Cookery, A Self-Guided Tour of Chatsworth and Vicinity, Churches and Graveyards of the Pine Barrens, The Bat Book, Piney Talk, Towns Lost but Not Forgotten, Folk Foods of the Pine Barrens*, and, in the future, hopefully *The Deer Hunting Clubs of the Pine Barrens*. These titles are in addition to a series of garden and seafood cookbooks and cookbooklets published under the imprint of *Barnegat Light Press*.

ACQUISITION

But back to Buzby's. I learned that the Buzby property had been lost by the owners for nonpayment of real estate taxes. The property had been leased to other people for several years, but somehow the taxes were not paid. I eventually learned that a Bordentown investment firm now owned the tax lien.

My first step was to find an attorney. This proved a major problem. After several rejections, primarily because Buzby's had sold gasoline and there were underground gas tanks, no attorney was interested. Local rumors were that there were tanks all over the property. With the advice and commiseration of a local cranberry grower, I finally engaged a local attorney. During this period, through friends in Barnegat Light, I learned of a local builder. His inspection and that of my brother, an engineer, confirmed that the structure was essentially sound and worth saving.

The attorney arranged for me to purchase the tax lien and begin foreclosure proceedings on the owners of record. This process required another attorney and took two years. After obtaining a clear title, I was ready for work.

During this two-year period, I had interviewed and finally hired a local carpenter to restore the building. The builder also secured the doors to Buzby's to prevent the local young people from gaining access. That they had been drinking and smoking in the building was evident by the rubble left behind. The builder aided me in securing the needed subcontractors—electricians, additional carpenters, plumbers, heating/air conditioning contractors, and other craftsmen as needed.

Buzby's Chatsworth General Store, 1992.

THE FIRE

Unfortunately, before I was able to obtain insurance on Buzby's, a major fire destroyed the adjacent garage and outhouse. A neighbor heard a popping noise and fortunately called the fire department. The garage and the outhouse were destroyed. The store remained undamaged mainly because of asbestos siding and the good work of the local fire departments. Eventually I obtained liability insurance through Lloyd's of London, the only firm that would cover an unoccupied historic site.

RESTORATION

Because of many rumors of tanks located throughout the property and the advice of my attorney, I hired an engineering firm to inspect the property. Sophisticated equipment was used to locate all underground tanks. Gasoline tanks were found along Route 563 and two tanks between the store and the remains of the burned garage.

June 1998.

June 1998: Gary Alloway discarding stumps he pulled out.

June 1998: Gutting the feed room.

July 1998: New studs for commercial kitchen, bath and mail rooms.

Although my foreclosure attorney felt that a survey was unnecessary, I felt it was—and it was! After the engineering firm and surveyors completed their work, it was discovered that the gasoline tanks were located on county property. My few years in real estate and as a tax assessor (CTA) paid off! This information was conveyed to the Woodland Township mayor with the request that corrective action be initiated. Copies of all information—survey and engineering reports—were submitted to him.

Restoration of Buzby's started with a major clean out and cleanup. A firm was hired to clean out the second floor of the store (the living quarters). At the foot of the attic stairs the bat droppings were 2 to 3 feet high! Protective suits and respirators were furnished to the clean-up crew. Bottles—whiskey, beer, etc.—were removed as were old carpets and linoleum flooring, revealing the original pine floors.

The builder and his crew cleaned out the first floor and basement. Pine paneling was removed and discarded as was the old kitchen equipment. Fortunately, a friend photographed all stages of the restoration.

Removal of the roof (multiple layers of wood and asbestos shingles) was delayed to give the numerous baby bats living in the attic time to mature and migrate. Since the building had been vacant for seven years, the bats had found a happy home and developed a maternity colony. Coping with them was rather staggering.

During replacement of the roof, a fire hatch located on the east side was preserved. This was an unusual finding in the pines. It provided access to the roof from the attic in the event of a fire.

To facilitate the removal of asbestos and aluminum siding, and replacement of the roof and windows, scaffolding was constructed. It attracted much attention and was frequently referred to as a work of art by other builders.

In the northwest room, previously a porch that at one time had been enclosed, was an impressive growth of green moss. Unfortunately, we failed to photograph it. It was somewhat overwhelming.

The store clean-out was another massive chore. All refrigeration units, meat display case, stove, and other storage racks were removed and discarded. A few tables and chairs were preserved. Removal of the dropped ceiling revealed scars of a fire—burned beams! I later learned this had been the location of a pot belly stove in the early days of the store. This stove had been surrounded by an iron wheel filled with sand—to collect tobacco juice spit by the locals! Each day brought new adventures. Removal of pine paneling revealed hidden doors and a window.

Because of the necessary redesign and new use of both floors, an architect was engaged to insure compliance with building codes and environmental regulations. A handicapped accessible restroom, a handicapped entrance ramp, and a commercial kitchen were needed. A café and gift shop area plus an office completed the first floor. The original Buzby candy counter and safe were preserved.

Consulting engineers hired to inspect the property located two areas containing underground tanks and estimated their size. A tank removal firm was engaged to remove the two tanks (oil?) located between the store and the remains of the burned garage. (This garage was the location for storing the body of the famous Mexican flier, Captain Emilio Carranza, after his plane crashed in

July 1998: Roof removal.

September 1998: Jack and Bill Fackler opening fireplace.

August 1998: Exterior completed.

the pines.) Excavation revealed one tank, long and narrow, which was bolted together! Wonder how old it was? Truckloads of contaminated soil were removed and properly remediated. Later testing revealed remnants of contaminated water. Testing two years later revealed existing contamination (according to revised DEP regulations). All work was performed in compliance with DEP regulations by a registered consulting firm. The six tanks located along Route 563 (east side) on county property remain.

For heating and air conditioning, a decision was made to install a geothermal system. Two wells (130 feet deep) were drilled in the western area of the property and heat exchangers installed on each floor. Water conditioning equipment was also installed in the basement. This approach seemed logical since the Pine Barrens are situated over millions of gallons of water. This also deleted the concern about hydrocarbon (oil) contamination and expense. Economy was also a guiding factor.

June 1998: Removal of tank #2.

1998: Drilling wells for geothermal system.

The second floor of the store, the original bedrooms (later living quarters), had a bathroom in the western hall. This was redesigned into a modern efficient kitchen, preserving the original door. The main room, referred to as the west bedroom, where Willis Jefferson Buzby died, was designed into a living-dining area.

Throughout the second floor the original wide pine floorboards (6-8 inches) were sanded and refinished. The bedrooms remained except for the southeastern wall, which had contained a staircase removed at some unknown time. The eastern bedroom was shortened and with the remaining staircase was converted into a large bathroom containing a stacked washer and drier, a linen tower, in addition to a large shower, sink, and toilet. The small western bedroom was converted into an office with extra wiring for computer and office equipment. In the south bedroom, space under the attic staircase was converted into a large closet.

The original west bedroom, which had a galley kitchen, was designed as a great room—living room, dining areas and kitchen. The existing fireplace had a new period-appropriate mantle installed; on the advice of masons, the chimney was blocked. The chimney flue serving the old heating system and fireplaces on each floor was not restored.

Rather than removing wallpaper and repairing the plaster walls, new sheetrock was installed to cover the old deteriorated plaster walls. New baseboards were installed where necessary.

Interestingly after obtaining title to the property, I arrived one morning to find six 55-gallon drums located by the east entrance. No one knew who had left them there. A call to the New Jersey State Police resulted in the arrival of two patrol cars, county health department personnel, a fire engine, and emergency management personnel! The intersection was illuminated with flashing lights—red, white, blue. No one had any answers. A trip to the local township offices revealed that PNC Bank had made inquiries about a general store in town. It seems that there had been two general stores in Chatsworth. The other one was located north of Buzby's and was known as Broom's General Store. PNC Bank had recently acquired title to the Broom property and had hired an environmental firm to empty the gasoline tanks. It appeared that they had emptied Buzby's by mistake—an expensive mistake! The environmental consultants were contacted and agreed to remove the drums within a reasonable time. The mystery was resolved.

During the major cleanup phase, a barn remaining on the west side of the property (the hay barn) was deemed unsalvageable. Since it was built of white cedar, the old siding was preserved and eventually used to rebuild the burned outhouse on its original site. The outhouse, which fortunately had been photographed before the fire, had a window and a two-hole seat. Mrs. Buzby had the reputation of having the cleanest outhouse in town—and with a white lace curtain in the window. This, too, was replaced. The remaining white cedar barn boards were donated to Whitesbog Village for restoration of their outhouses. Old signs stored in the barn were preserved and installed on the walls of the café area.

The sidewalk along First Avenue was totally deteriorated. It was replaced at my expense prior to opening the store.

The first floor of the store, designed to contain a café, handicapped accessible restroom, gift shop, commercial kitchen, and an office, had a handicapped accessible entrance provided on the south wall leading to the handicapped accessible ramp and the designated parking area.

The majority of the floors on the first floor were in poor condition and had to be replaced. An access hole had to be cut in the original flooring to remove 55-gallon drums remaining in the basement. Floors were replaced with wide pine flooring in the café area. The entrance hall floor was identified as maple and refinished. The gift shop area had a new plywood floor covered with carpeting.

At one time the basement access was by Bilco-style doors on the outside of the east wall and by an interior staircase on the south wall. A trap door existed in the café area floor where an original staircase existed. The staircase, leading to the second floor and basement, had

The original candy counter at Buzby's.

been removed at some unknown time. In the early days of the store, kerosene was sold in the store. The storage drums for it remained in the basement, as did miscellaneous metal storage racks.

It should be noted that the basement also contained the original coalbin and a large coal furnace. Multiple

wells were present; these had furnished water to the store and living quarters.

During restoration, it was necessary to have a water supply. One of the wells was put back into operation. To accomplish this, a neighbor, a renowned well expert, was called into service. He "shot" my well! Needless to say, I was more than a little startled when he came from the basement announcing that he "shot" my well and it now worked fine. It seems that a well is really shot to loosen the corrosion. This well worked fine as long as it was needed.

In the café area, transom windows on the east wall, which had been replaced with plywood, were rebuilt and replaced. Beadboard paneling was installed to chair rail height. The bay window, lined with pegboard inside and aluminum siding outside, was restored by removing these

The Evolution of Buzby's restoration.

items and eventually protecting the original windows with interior storm windows.

The storefront porch had been replaced with brick sometime in the 1970s or 1980s. This brickwork was removed and the porch restored to the original conformation with a mahogany deck (installed with brass marine screws for looks!).

Renovation of the original west room, intended for use as a gift shop, revealed two doors leading to the front entrance hall. These doors were preserved. The original candy counter dating back to the 1800s was moved to this area and restored. The fireplace, which had been bricked closed, was opened to reveal a chimney going to the coal furnace in the basement. The mantle was missing and eventually replaced by one of an appropriate period style. Interestingly, the masons explained that the bricks were handmade and one contained a footprint of a raccoon. A stovepipe outlet to vent a pot belly stove used for heating in the early days remains above the mantle.

Throughout the building, new energy efficient windows replaced the deteriorated existing ones. New exterior doors were installed with the exception of the

September 19, 1999: Crowd filing into newly renovated store on Buzby's grand opening.

main store entrance door. A new roof of composite shingles replaced the existing one. The original large windows in the café area remained. All asbestos and aluminum siding on the exterior of the building was removed so that the original white cedar siding could be restored or replaced as needed.

Little was done to the basement. Water conditioning and geothermal system equipment were installed here. The remaining coalbin was preserved as was the coal chute on the western porch. Interestingly, the private entrance on the west side of the building led to a hall with a beautiful maple floor. This hall led to the upstairs staircase, the first-floor office, and the entrance to the basement.

Moving

On December 24, 1998, I moved in! Prior to this, I was living temporarily in my brother's home in Barnegat Light. An unexpected snowstorm convinced me and Pumpkin cat to move to Chatsworth even though I had not received my occupancy permit. Fortunately, the snowstorm only involved Long Beach Island and did not reach Chatsworth.

After I settled in the apartment, a friend, Captain Lou Puskas of Barnegat Light, presented me with the original outhouse seat—a house warming gift—which today is preserved on the wall of the handicapped restroom (see page 77). Note the width of the seat board. An archaeologist deemed this a significant treasure that should be preserved.

The Barn

Early in the restoration process I contracted for a 30 x 50 ft. Morton's metal pole barn to replace the burned garage. This was needed for book storage and garage, and eventually a conference center. The barn was erected in two days. Then the concrete floor was poured and waterproofed. Pegboard was installed in the garage area and a cage constructed at a later date for book storage.

Grand Opening

Members of the community watched the restoration of Buzby's with awe. Many stopped to view the progress. One of the most pleasant memories happened as the painters were hard at work. Mr. and Mrs. Charles Applegate, lifelong friends of Katie Buzby, stopped to watch the work. When I asked them what they thought, after a moment's hesitation Mr. Applegate said, "Katie is smiling!" Katie had died recently; she had spent her last days in a Medford nursing home after moving from her home across the street from the store. How sad that she was not able to enjoy the restoration of the general store.

A grand opening was planned. Invitations were issued to friends, relatives, and all folks on the local mailing list, approximately 700! On opening day, the mayor cut the ribbon, officially opening Buzby's for business. Cake and cranberry lemonade were served to over 700 visitors who signed the guest book. The following day Buzby's café and gift shop, The Cheshire Cat, opened for business. Special mugs featuring Buzby's store had been produced. They are still in demand today.

The café served breakfast and lunch. Unfortunately, Pine Barrens products were not on the menu. The gift shop featured publications related to the Pine Barrens and coastal area, in addition to foods such as jams, jellies, cranberry and blueberry muffin and pancake mixes. Artwork by Pine Barrens artists decorated the walls. Other miscellaneous gift items related to the Pine Barrens supplemented the inventory.

CAFÉ HISTORY

My first adventure as a café landlord was a disaster, resulting in filing for eviction against my tenant who fortunately left at the end of her three-year lease.

After that incident, I expanded my gift shop into the café area. This worked well, but a café was really needed in this area. Several years later, I was approached to lease the café again. Since local residents and tourists needed a place for a cup of coffee, I agreed to a one-year lease. This tenant lasted 11 months! He was dissatisfied because I wouldn't let him sell t-shirts! A café is definitely needed in this area. It was unfortunate since this tenant was a good cook but other factors in his life impinged on his decisions.

Fortunately, it was easy to expand the gift shop into the café area. The gift shop, the Cheshire Cat, was named after the cat in Alice in Wonderland because sometimes the shop is open, sometimes not! I appear and disappear. It works well.

TANK PROBLEM

Although everyone in Chatsworth seemed to know about the underground gasoline tanks at Buzby's, no one could offer conclusive details. My consulting engineers located the tanks, number, size, etc. After pressuring the local mayor for action, he responded by contacting the county officials. A meeting arranged in Mt. Holly at the county offices was attended by the Woodland Township mayor, two county attorneys, the county administrator, a freeholder, and me. The freeholder explained that my restoration of Buzby's was greatly appreciated since the store was a county landmark, and that the county had agreed to pay ⅓ the cost of the tank removal, the township of Woodland ⅓, and me to pay the remainder—and also that I would be the general contractor. Papers were pushed to me to sign. As I returned them to one of the county attorneys, I explained that I couldn't sign them since they owned the land—I didn't! The county attorney, needless to say, was somewhat upset. I informed him that I had turned all documents over to the mayor concerning the fact that the county owned the property containing the tanks. The meeting was promptly adjourned with the county attorney stating that he had to do research.

A prompt call to my foreclosure attorney brought him up to date on the happenings. My attorney was contacted by the county attorney (this was his research) who advised that a 100-year title search confirmed that the county owned the property; I didn't!

Eventually the county contracted to remove the tanks (8 based on their data). The county and I had an agreement (in writing) giving them permission to use my land as necessary for the tank removal but also requiring them to restore the land to its original condition. By this time, I had installed fencing and landscaped the area.

The contractors then asked where in my yard they could dump the contaminated soil. I replied that they couldn't without putting up a bond and having a written agreement with me. Since then multiple letters (including registered ones) to the freeholder remain unanswered. The project died. In 2013 the county road department repaved Route 563 over the tanks. The tanks remain in situ. No response was ever received from the freeholder (who is no longer in office).

HISTORIC SITE DESIGNATION

Documents from Buzby's Chatsworth General Store, including purchase orders, family death certificates, correspondence, etc., have been transferred to Stockton University. They are housed in the South Jersey Special Collections of the Bjork Library as the Buzby-Schmidt Collection.

Albert Morison, leader of restoration team, reading an old artifact found on site.

Neither local recognition of Buzby's General Store as a historic site nor John McPhee's designation of the store as Capital of the Pines in *The Pine Barrens* was official. To obtain designation as an official state and federal historic site, it was necessary to apply to the New Jersey Historic Preservation Office. Not knowing architectural terminology, I registered for appropriate courses at Burlington County College. After two years of courses, I applied to the state office for a Certificate of Eligibility (COE).

Throughout the restoration, all existing conditions and changes (restoration) were documented photographically from the time the store was acquired to its complete restoration. These photographs proved invaluable in preparing both the COE forms and the application for listing Buzby's in the National Register of Historic Places. Fortunately, the COE application received approval after several edits.

The next step was to complete the National Register application. This application was more intensive, requiring the same photographic documentation of all modifications to the building since construction as well as historic photographs obtained from local residents and literature about the area.

As a result of successfully completing the National Register nomination, Buzby's gained its listing in the New Jersey State Register of Historic Places on January 16, 2004, and in the National Register of Historic Places on March 25, 2004. A plaque mounted on the fireplace marks this official designation.

In 2013 Buzby's Chatsworth General Store was offered for sale. To date (2017) no sale has been completed.

Historic documents from Buzby's Chatsworth General Store. Images from top left to bottom right: wholesale grocery invoice; mailing envelope from The Edgewater Flour Mill Company; receipt from the Central Railroad Company of New Jersey; an original invoice from, at the time, the Standard Oil Company, now ExxonMobil. *Courtesy of the Buzby-Schmidt Collection, Special Collections and Archives, the Richard E. Bjork Library, Stockton University.*

R. Marilyn Schmidt, the most recent owner of Buzby's Chatworth General Store, lighting up the room with her smile.

The original outhouse seat.

The Publications of R. Marilyn Schmidt

As of June 17, 2017

Since 1980, Marilyn Schmidt has been researching, writing, often illustrating, and publishing titles related to the Jersey Shore and nearby Pine Barrens. The majority of her publications are cookbooks detailing seafood recipes—Marilyn tested and perfected each recipe in her own kitchen. Her cookbooklets, 5.5 x 8.5" pamphlet bound titles, provide excellent, brief introductions to unfamiliar dishes. Her longer cookbooks and books on gardening and the Pine Barrens provide in-depth discussions of the topic under consideration. Sixty-nine titles are listed in this bibliography; undoubtedly, a few titles have eluded our search.

COOKBOOKLETS BY BARNEGAT LIGHT PRESS

All About Monkfish, Barnegat Light Press, 1982.

Everything You Always Wanted to Know About Tilefish, Barnegat Light Press, 1982.

Bluefish: A Cookbooklet, Barnegat Light Press, 1984.

Mussels: A Cookbooklet, Barnegat Light Press, 1984, 1989, 2011.

Fresh Tuna: A Cookbooklet, Barnegat Light Press, 1985, 1994, 2000.

Mackerel: A Cookbooklet, Barnegat Light Press, 1985, 1989.

R. Marilyn Schmidt cooking. *Courtesy of Renee Kennedy.*

The Publications of R. Marilyn Schmidt

Mako Shark: A Cookbooklet, Barnegat Light Press, 1985.

Soft Shell Clams, Steamers: A Cookbooklet, Barnegat Light Press, 1985.

Squid: A Cookbooklet, Barnegat Light Press, 1985, 1988.

And More Squid: A Cookbooklet, Barnegat Light Press, 1985.

Tilefish: A Cookbooklet, Barnegat Light Press, 1985, 1993.

Blue Crab: A Cookbooklet, Barnegat Light Press, 1986, 1989, 1994, 1997.

Eastern Oysters: A Cookbooklet, Barnegat Light Press, 1986, 1989.

Swordfish: A Cookbooklet, Barnegat Light Press, 1986, 1989.

Weakfish, Sea Trout: A Cookbooklet, Barnegat Light Press, 1986.

Flounder and Other Flat Fish: A Cookbooklet, Barnegat Light Press, 1987.

Scallops: A Cookbooklet, Barnegat Light Press, 1987, 1990.

Fresh Salmon: A Cookbooklet, Barnegat Light Press, 1988, 1994.

Hard Clams: A Cookbooklet, Barnegat Light Press, 1988.

Mahi-Mahi Dolphin: A Cookbooklet, Barnegat Light Press, 1988, 1993, 1995.

North American Lobster: A Cookbooklet, Barnegat Light Press, 1988.

Orange Roughy: A Cookbooklet, Barnegat Light Press, 1988, 1993, 1995.

Blackfish, Tautog: A Cookbooklet, Barnegat Light Press, 1989.

Shad – Shad-Roe: A Cookbooklet, Barnegat Light Press, 1989.

Cod, Pollock: A Cookbooklet, Barnegat Light Press, 1991, 2012.

Sea Bass: A Cookbooklet, Barnegat Light Press, 1991, 2012.

Sturgeon: A Cookbooklet, Barnegat Light Press, 1992.

Seafood Chowders, Soups, Bisques: A Cookbooklet, 2nd edition, Barnegat Light Press, 1995.

Seafood Stir-Fry: A Cookbooklet, Barnegat Light Press, 1995.

Tilipia – St. Peter's Fish: A Cookbooklet, Barnegat Light Press, 1996. [*Tilipia* on cover; *Tilapia* in text.]

Seafood Salads, Barnegat Light Press, 1997.

BARNEGAT LIGHT PRESS (NOT COOKBOOKLETS)

The Simply Seafood Cookbook of East Coast Fish, Barnegat Light Press, 1980.

The Simply Seafood Cookbook of East Coast Shellfish, Barnegat Light Press, 1980, 1983, 1987, 1994.

Seafood Secrets: A Nutritional Guide to Seafood: Recipes for Finfish and Shellfish, Barnegat Light Press, 1982.

Gardening on the Eastern Seashore, Barnegat Light Press, 1983, 1989, 1993, 1997; republished by Pine Barrens Press, 2005.

All About Blueberries, Barnegat Light Press, 1985.

All About Caviar, Barnegat Light Press, 1985.

Cooking the Shore Catch, Barnegat Light Press, 1986, 2002.

Revised Seafood Secrets: A Nutritional Guide to Seafood, Barnegat Light Press, second edition, 1986.

Bargain Seafoods: How to Cook the Underutilized Species, Barnegat Light Press, 1987.

Seafood: Smoking, Grilling, Barbecuing, Barnegat Light Press, 1987, 1998.

Simply Shrimp, Barnegat Light Press, 1988.

How to Shuck an Oyster, Barnegat Light Press, 1989.

Beach Plum Jelly / Rose Hip Jam and Other Favorites, Barnegat Light Press, 1993, 1997, 2012.

A Sampler of Canned Seafoods, Barnegat Light Press, 1994.

Herb-Flavored Oils & Butters, Barnegat Light Press, 1995, 1997.

PINE BARRENS PRESS

Cranberry Cookery, Pine Barrens Press, a Division of Barnegat Light Press, 1985; *Cranberry Cookery II*, 1991; *Cranberry Cookery Complete*, 1998.

Flavored Vinegars: Herb and Fruit, Pine Barrens Press, a Division of Barnegat Light Press, 1988, 1993.

Herb Sauces, Salsas and Such, Pine Barrens Press, a Division of Barnegat Light Press, 1991, 1993, 1997.

A Guide to New Jersey's Lighthouses, Pine Barrens Press, a Division of Barnegat Light Press, 1992, 1993, 2000.

Mustard Magic!, Pine Barrens Press, a Division of Barnegat Light Press, 1992.

The Best of Blueberry Cookery, Pine Barrens Press, a Division of Barnegat Light Press, 1993, 2003.

Seashore Plants by Mail, Pine Barrens Press, a Division of Barnegat Light Press, 1993.

Chutney Complete, Pine Barrens Press, a Division of Barnegat Light Press, 1994.

Gardening in the Pinelands, Pine Barrens Press, a Division of Barnegat Light Press, 1994. (Two printings 1994.)

How to Write and Publish a Family Cookbook, Pine Barrens

Press, a Division of Barnegat Light Press, 1995.

Exploring the Pine Barrens: A Guide, Pine Barrens Press, a Division of Barnegat Light Press, 1997, 2000, 2003.

Exploring the Pine Barrens: A Map, Pine Barrens Press, a Division of Barnegat Light Press, 1997, 2000.

Seashore Gardening with Native Plants, Pine Barrens Press, a Division of Barnegat Light Press, 1997.

The Bat Book, Pine Barrens Press, a Division of Barnegat Light Press, 1999.

Wines and Wineries of New Jersey: A Guide, Pine Barrens Press, a Division of Barnegat Light Press, 2000.

Piney Talk: What Does a Piney Mean When He Says . . ., Pine Barrens Press, a Division of Barnegat Light Press, 2001, 2012.

A Self-Guided Tour of Chatsworth & Vicinity, Pine Barrens Press, a Division of Barnegat Light Press, 2001.

Churches & Graveyards of the Pine Barrens of New Jersey, Pine Barrens Press, a Division of Barnegat Light Press, 2002.

Towns Lost But Not Forgotten in the Pine Barrens of New Jersey, Pine Barrens Press, a Division of Barnegat Light Press, 2004, 2012.

Folk Food of the Pine Barrens of New Jersey, Pine Barrens Press, a Division of Barnegat Light Press, 2006, 2012. [*Food* on cover; *Foods* in text.]

The Rebirth of Buzby's Chatsworth General Store, Pine Barrens Press, a Division of Barnegat Light Press, 2016, 2017.

The Clevengers: Glass Masters. A Brief History, Pine Barrens Press, a Division of Barnegat Light Press, 2017.

OTHER PUBLISHERS

R. Marilyn Schmidt and Solomon Margolin, *Harper's Handbook of Therapeutic Pharmacology*, Philadelphia: Harper and Row, 1981.

R. Marilyn Schmidt selling her books. *Courtesy of Renee Kennedy.*

The Endicott-Reardon Family Museum

Rebecca Muller

In the hustle and bustle of today's society, we often neglect to appreciate the history that surrounds us, especially here in Southern New Jersey, where old dirt roads and farmland have been transformed into paved, main roads and new, busy store strips. In Seaville, Cape May County, just off of Route 9, sits The Endicott-Reardon Family Museum. It is South Jersey's time machine.

While many of us keep important family artifacts or old photographs of loved ones, few family collections can match the depth of detail, the amount of documentation, and the preservation of past materials that survive in this museum. Harriett Reardon Bailey, museum owner and proud descendant of the Endicott and Reardon families, admits that she has always held onto things, ever since

she can remember. For many years she has been dedicated to preserving the lives of her family by collecting their belongings. Small collections that started in her home are transformed into the home-style exhibits which grace the museum building today, a newly built structure modeled after her family's bungalow. Visitors will agree that Harriett's efforts have paid off in preserving and presenting her family's artifacts as a generous slice of middle-class life in South Jersey.

Upon entering the museum, visitors are struck by the richness of life that existed during the 1920s and 1930s in Seaville, but also by its simplicity. Take the tour with Harriett and you will feel as though you have stepped back in time to the period when her family owned and worked the land upon which the museum is located.

The Endicott-Reardon Family Museum, April 3, 2017.

Harriett pointing to workers, including her father, at the American Store in Sea Isle City, today's Acme.

The museum's living room display featuring furniture, decor, books, and light fixtures owned by family members.

The Endicott-Reardon Family Museum

The special exhibit room dedicated to the dolls Harriett has collected throughout her life.

The collection portrays intimate aspects of life in both the Endicott and Reardon families. Artifacts, memorabilia, and pieces of everyday life are displayed. Visitors glimpse fragments of past lifestyles and gain insight into the history of hard working, middle-class families in South Jersey. Organized like the original homes of her family, space in the museum is separated into sections resembling a parlor, kitchen, dining room, bedroom, and a child's playroom. Other sections include exhibits on schoolwork, community life, work life, the military, and a special exhibit dedicated to the dolls Harriett has collected throughout her life.

The museum chronicles the day-to-day lives of both families, the circumstances behind their arrival in South Jersey, and the legacy they left behind as hardworking contributors to their community.

The exhibits are representative of commonplace life during the 1920s and 1930s in South Jersey. Family members were involved in the many different facets of the local community including school teaching, store management, raising children (and chickens), military service, and involvement in church and public events. Exhibits describe a lifestyle of both hard work and leisure for those living close to but not quite on the Shore. Overall, exhibits stress the love and close connections of family.

The attractiveness of the museum derives from its intimacy and relatability. These families were everyday people working everyday jobs in order to raise their children and make comfortable lives for themselves. By documenting and preserving her family history, Harriett provides a window that looks back to a very local past.

The museum is located at 3036 S. Shore Road (Route 9) in Seaville, NJ 08230. Visitors are welcome on Mondays, Fridays, and Saturdays from 10am – 2pm.

Phone: (609) 624-0600
Email: info@ermuseum.com

A variety of collectibles.

More Recent Publications

Swan Bay Jim / Gasoline Seventeen Cents a Gallon; Moonshine a Dollar a Quart
by Gary B. Giberson

Gary B. Giberson, Mayor of Port Republic, New Jersey, for over three decades, is a master decoy carver, entrepreneur, and now, author. His work betrays a lifelong love of the pines—no surprise, given his strong ancestral ties to the Ocean / Atlantic county region dating from as early as the seventeenth century.

Two short stories, with illustrations by distinguished artist Kathy Anne English and photographs courtesy of Giberson. Escape the modern-day commotion and follow an impossible hunt through the cedar swamps of the Mullica River and on an adventurous chase to capture rum-runners during Prohibition.
40 pages, paperback
ISBN: 978-0-9976699-4-7
$5.00

Burlington Biographies: A History of Burlington, New Jersey, Told Through the Lives and Times of Its People
by Robert L. Thompson

This study takes a fresh look at the history of Burlington, New Jersey, its rich heritage and longstanding lore. Sometimes it supports and strengthens well-known historical accounts; other times it topples commonly held myths that extend back a century or more. The book will delight, entertain, and intrigue both the reader who possesses knowledge of Burlington and the neophyte who seeks to learn more about this community settled by intrepid Quakers in the second half of the seventeenth century. Topics include African American history, the American War for Independence, architecture, artisanal work, city planning, immigration, merchants, and prior local historians, among a host of others. Readers are invited to find a comfortable chair and immerse themselves in the Burlington of yesteryear. Publication of this title was partially supported by a grant from the New Jersey Historical Commission.
558 pages, hardcover with dust jacket
ISBN: 978-0-9888731-9-3
$29.95

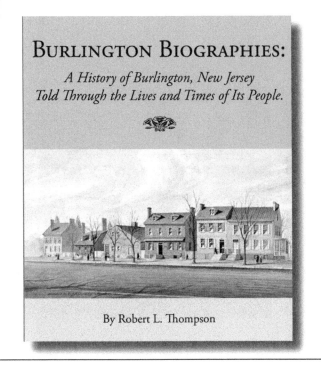

Anecdotes and Memoirs of William Boen

1834

INTRODUCTION

Anecdotes and Memoirs of William Boen is a brief pamphlet originally published in 1834. The text, reproduced here, focuses on the life of William Boen, an African American man born into slavery in 1735 near Rancocas, Burlington County, New Jersey, who became a Quaker by lifestyle and, as an elderly man, through membership. Little biographical information exists for Boen beyond this text; hence, *Anecdotes* serves as a vital document both in understanding Boen's life and introducing the issues surrounding African Americans and slavery relative to Quakerism in South Jersey.

The first part of *Anecdotes* features an interview between Boen and an unidentified Quaker, providing Boen's answers to questions about his life and his faith. This section also features the unnamed author's commentary on Boen's responses. The second part of this text features posthumous testimonies of Boen's life by members of the Religious Society of Friends during a meeting in Mount Holly, New Jersey, held in April 1828 and approved at a Burlington Quarterly Meeting held in Chesterfield, New Jersey, during November of the same year. Both parts of this brief text present Boen as an admirable man whose faith served as an example to all Quakers. While the text focuses mainly on Boen's devotion to religion, there are indications of pro-abolition views throughout the document.

William Boen is iconic of the myriad complex paradoxes within slavery, race relations, and equity facing white people of faith in general, and specifically those who held membership in the Religious Society of Friends (Quakers) during the eighteenth and early nineteenth centuries. Born into slavery in 1735, Boen awakened to his Christian faith while in his twenties as he worked on clearing a hilltop for his master, Moses Haines, of Springfield Township, Burlington County. He was devout in his newfound faith and followed the precepts and tenets of the Friends. Quaker abolitionist John Woolman befriended him and provided guidance to Boen in his Christian walk.

In 1763, Boen, desirous of wedding a free woman of color named Dido in a Quaker ceremony, applied to the Mount Holly Friends' Meeting for membership and for the marriage to occur under the meeting's aegis. The meeting deliberated over the application, but then rejected it, since the meeting "accepted no negro members."[1] Woolman expressed dismay at the handling of Boen's application. As the authors of *Fit for Freedom, Not for Friendship* noted, "Woolman, disturbed at the delay in responding to Boen, predicted correctly that the meeting would 'dwindle and become reduced again' because it was unwilling to see the African American as an equal."[2] Following the initial rejection, Woolman personally nominated Boen to be an elder in the meeting, but his efforts met with the same negative results. To fulfill Boen's wishes, Woolman drafted a proper Quaker marriage certificate and, under his authority as a Public Friend (minister), called a worship meeting and marriage ceremony at a private residence, probably that of Joseph Burr, Dido's employer and Woolman's cousin.

Despite rejection at the hands of the Mount Holly Meeting, Boen dressed and spoke in the way of Quakers, eschewing, like Woolman, any article of clothing associated with slavery. Two years after his marriage, Boen was manumitted by Moses Haines. He joined Woolman in becoming an outspoken advocate for abolition, particularly among Quakers, at a time prior to the sect reaching a consensus concerning owning another human being. Despite his piety, Boen lived almost his entire life as a Quaker standing outside the meetinghouse looking in, but he held no animosity for those who affronted him with racial animus. Rather, he defeated their sense of superiority with pure Christian love. Mount Holly Meeting finally granted his petition for membership in 1814, a mere ten years before his death. Had the local Quakers finally accepted African Americans as equals; or did they admit Boen to full membership in the meeting under a sense of duty? It is up to the reader to determine the answer to this question, for the answer goes to the very heart of the paradoxes mentioned above.

By Elizabeth M. Birch and Paul W. Schopp

ANECDOTES AND MEMOIRS
OF WILLIAM BOEN

William Boen was a coloured man, who resided near Mount Holly, New Jersey. Like many of his brethren of the African race, in those days, he was from his birth held as a slave. But though poor and ignorant, in his early days, he was cared for, as all others are, by the universal Parent of the human family. He became a pious, sober, temperate, honest, and industrious man; and by this means, he obtained the friendship, esteem, and respect of all classes of his fellow men, and the approbation and peace of his heavenly Father.

His industry, temperance, and cleanliness, no doubt, contributed much to his health and comfort; so that he lived to be a very old man, with having but little sickness through the course of his life. His character being so remarkable for sobriety, honesty, and peace—that it induced some younger people to inquire by what means he had arrived to such a state, and attained such a standing in the neighbourhood where he lived. Ever willing to instruct, counsel, and admonish the youth, he could relate his own experience of the work of grace in his heart, which led him into such uprightness of life and conduct. For his memory did not appear to be much impaired by reason of old age.

To a friend who visited him in the eighty-sixth year of his age, he gave the following account of his early life, and religious experience. On being asked, whether he could remember in what way, and by what means, he was first brought to mind and follow *that*, which had been his guide and rule of faith and life, and which had led and preserved him so safely along through time? William answered as follows: "Oh! yes; that I can, right well. In the time of the old French war, my master (for I was a poor black boy, a slave) my master sent me to chop wood, on a hill-side, out of sight of any house; and there was a great forest of woods below me; and he told me to cut down all the trees on that hill-side. When I went home, in the evenings, I often heard them talking about the Indians killing and scalping people: and sometimes, some of the neighbours would come in, and they and my master's family talked of the Indians killing such and such,—nearer and nearer to us. And so, from time to time, I would hear them tell of the Indians killing, and scalping people, nearer and nearer: so that I began to think, like enough, by and by, they would kill me. And I thought more and more about it; and again would hear tell of their coming still nearer. At length, I thought, sure enough they will get so near, that they will hear the sound of my axe, and will come and kill me. Here is a great forest of woods below me, and no house in sight:—surely, I have not long to live. I expected every day would be my last;—that they would soon kill me, a poor black boy, here all alone."

"A thought then came into my mind, whether I was fit to die. It was showed me, and I saw plain enough, that I was not fit to die. Then it troubled me very much, that I was not fit to die; and I felt very desirous,—very anxious that I might be made fit to die. So I stood still, in great amazement; and it seemed as if a flaming sword passed through me. And when it passed over, and I recollected myself (for I stood so, some time) it was showed me how I should be made fit to die: and I was willing to do any thing, so I might be made fit to die."

"Thus, I was brought to mind and follow *that*, that has been the guide and rule of my life,—*that within me*, that inclined me to good, and showed and condemned evil. Now I considered I had a new master—I had two masters; and it was showed me (in my mind) by my new Master, a certain tree on the hill-side, that I must not cut down. I knowed the tree well enough. I had not come to it yet. But I did not know what I *should* do; for my old master had told me to cut all the trees down, on that hill-side. My new Master forbids me to cut a certain one. So I thought a good deal about it. I cut on; and by and by I came to the tree. I cut on by it, and let it stand. But I expected, every day, my old master would come, and see that tree standing, and say, 'What did thee leave that tree standing for? Did not I tell thee to cut all the trees down, as thee went? Go, cut that tree down.' Then, I didn't know what I *should* do. But he never said any thing to me about it. I cut on, and got some distance by it; and one day my old master brought out his axe, and cut the tree down himself; and never said, William, why didn't thee cut that tree down? never said any thing to me about it. Then I thought, surely my new Master will make way for me, and take care of me, if I love him, and mind him, and am attentive to this my guide, and rule of life. And this seemed an evidence and proof of it, and strengthened me much in love, and confidence in my Guide."

After the respectable and goodly old man had given this interesting account of the way and manner in which he was brought to follow the guide of his life, the following question was put to him: "Well, William, has thee, from that time, till now, been so careful and attentive to thy guide, as never to say or do amiss?" To which he replied, "Oh! no: I have missed it—I have several times missed it." He was then asked, "Well, William, in that case, how *did* thee get along?" He answered, "Oh! when I missed it,—when I found I had said, or done wrong, I felt very sorry. I tried to be more careful, for time to come;—never to do so any more: and I believe I was forgiven."

Another inquiry was made of William, how he and his old master got along together, after his change. He said, "Very well. Some time afterwards, one of the

ANECDOTES AND MEMOIRS

OF

WILLIAM BOEN,

A COLOURED MAN,

WHO LIVED AND DIED NEAR MOUNT HOLLY, NEW JERSEY.

TO WHICH IS ADDED,

The Testimony of Friends of Mount Holly monthly meeting concerning him.

———

Philadelphia:

PRINTED BY JOHN RICHARDS,

No. 129 North Third Street.

1834.

Title page of *Anecdotes and Memoirs of William Boen.*

neighbours said to me, one day, 'William, thy master talks of setting thee free.' I didn't think much about it—didn't expect there was any thing in it; though I heard others say he talked of setting me free;—till, after some time, as my master was walking with me, going to my work, he said, 'William, wouldn't thee like to be free?' I didn't say any thing to it. I thought he might know I should like to be free. I didn't make him any answer about it, but then I thought there was something in it. So after awhile, sure enough, he did set me free." There is no doubt his old master observed a great change in him; for his guide taught him to be dutiful, industrious and diligent in his business, careful in his words and actions, and sober, steady, and exemplary in all he said, and in all his conduct.

William Boen's guide, and rule of life and conduct, his *new Master*, as he called him, that did so much for him, and raised him from the state of a poor slave, to be a free man, in good esteem—thro' habits of temperance, sobriety, honest industry and integrity,—whereby he was enabled to become the respectable head of a family, and to acquire a house, and property of his own, sufficient for the comfortable accommodation of himself and family;—and who forsook him not when he became old, and grey-headed;—his new Master was the same Light that appears unto all; and it would guide every one in the right way, as it did him, if they would take it for their Master, and mind and obey it, as he did. It was the guide of his youth,—became his Lord and Master, preserved him from evil,—and conducted him safely through the trials of life, to a good old age.

William Boen's new Master was, and is the same thing that the apostle Paul, in his Epistle to Titus, bears testimony to, in these words; "the grace of God, that bringeth salvation, hath appeared to all men;—teaching us, that, denying all ungodliness and worldly lusts, we should live soberly, righteously, and godly in this present world." Now, surely, if we don't take it for our master, and mind its teachings, we cannot *know* it to bring our salvation, or *save us* from *all ungodliness* and *worldly lusts*, as he did, and as all do, that are obedient to this grace of God, *the Light of Christ, within.*

In William Boen's simple account of the way and means, by which he was showed how he should be made fit to die;—that is, by minding and following *that within* him, which inclined him to good, and that showed and condemned him for evil,—the goodness, mercy, and condescending care of the Almighty Father, are striking-ly manifest. How graciously he suits his dispensations to the weak and ignorant states of his children, who sincerely seek him, and inquire what they shall do to be saved! When William Boen thought of death, some-thing showed him he was not fit to die. He "saw it plain

enough," and was troubled. In his anxiety to be prepared to die, he became still and quiet—and then he felt con-demnation, as a flaming sword, pass through him. When this had its effect to bring him to a state of humility and watchfulness, the Divine Light in his soul showed him the way in which he should walk, in order to become fit to die. He became willing to do any thing required of him: so, to prove his obedience, it was showed him, by his new Master, that he must leave a certain tree stand-ing, where he was felling timber. He began to reason upon consequences, but resolved to obey his new Master, in preference to his old one. It was sufficient to test his faith and love; and though a simple circumstance, it was probably of great use to him ever after; as by it he was taught to be faithful in little things, and thus became ruler over more.

It may be useful to survivors, who, like William, are desirous so to live, as that they may become fit to die,—to bring into view some anecdotes of his life, that show the principles by which his mind and conduct were regulated.

In his conversation among men, he was very careful to keep to the plain language,—the language of truth and sincerity—yet, through the help of his guide, he detected himself in a deviation from it, in the following circumstance. A wealthy neighbour, a white man, frequently availed himself of William's obliging disposition, by using his grindstone, instead of procuring one for himself. On an occasion of this kind, his neighbour told him he was obliged to him for the use of his grindstone: to which, William returned the usual compliment of saying he was welcome. After the man was gone, William became uneasy in his mind, with his reply, as being insincere. He therefore went to his neighbour, and made an acknowledgment, that although he had told him he was welcome, yet it was only in conformity with custom, and was not the case; for he thought his neighbour was better able to keep a grindstone of his own, than he was.

How many customary compliments, by-words, and common expressions, would be dispensed with, as idle words, for which we must give an account in the day of judgment,—if a strict regard to truth and sincerity, were the ruling principle or guide of all our words and actions!

William Boen appears to have been as strictly careful in his adherence to the principles of justice, and the rights of property, as he was in regard to truth and sincerity in his communications. Being employed, with several others, to mow the meadows attached to the place called Breezy Ridge, on Lomberton creek,—William, with his scythe, accidentally struck a partridge that was concealed from his view, in the grass, and killed it. As it appeared to be in good order, his companions proposed that he should take it home, for his own use. William, however, was not easy to do so: he said the partridge did not belong to him, but to the owner of the meadow.

On another occasion, he manifested the acuteness of his feelings, in regard to the rights of property. With other labourers, he was employed to cut timber in the pines, at a distance from the settlements. They took provisions with them, to encamp for a week or two in the woods; and, finding an empty cabin on lands that did not belong to their employer, they made use of it. William's mind, however, was not quite satisfied. He had been using the property of another, without leave. So, after his return, he took an early opportunity to represent the case to the owner of the cabin, who lived some miles distant from him.

William Boen believed in Christ, as the Prince of peace; and that those who professed to be Christians, and lived in his peaceable spirit, could have nothing to do with war, in any shape. He therefore had a testimony to bear against the spirit of war, and the love of money that stands in connexion with it. Not far from William's habitation, there lived a storekeeper, a man of considerable note, who had been an officer in the army, during the time of the American revolution. Some time after the peace was concluded, this storekeeper traded largely in buying up soldiers' certificates, for much less than their nominal value. By this means, he made considerable profits to himself, with which he engaged in building a large and fine house. While thus employed, William Boen called on him, and told him he had been much concerned for him, on account of his traffic in what he considered no better than the price of blood, and that the money with which he was building his house, was unrighteous gain. He also quoted that passage of scripture, as applicable to the case, respecting Judas, who betrayed his Master for the sake of money; and mentioned the manner of his death.

His reproof and admonition were delivered with so much honesty and tender feeling, and the kind and friendly motives that influenced him thereto, were so apparent, that his neighbour, though a high-spirited man, received his communication, in a respectful manner;—and, on a subsequent occasion, upon hearing some persons remark, that they wondered that William was not ridiculed by boys, and light, vain persons, on account of his singular appearance, and wearing his beard so long,—he stated, that William Boen was a religious man; and that his well-known piety impressed the minds of such people with awe and respect towards him; and thus they were prevented from manifesting that levity which the singularity of his dress and appearance might otherwise have produced.

For it is to be observed, that he thought it right to have all his clothing of the natural colours, and made very plain and simple. As he was very clean in his person, his wearing apparel became very white, by washing—his hair and beard also became white through age: and these, contrasted with his dark skin, gave him a very venerable appearance. He was affable, modest, and respectful, in his manners and deportment; while the mildness and gravity of his countenance, indicated a mind governed by the precepts of the gospel, and often impressed lessons of serious reflection on those who beheld him;—especially in the solidity and reverence, with which he sat in religious meetings.

It was probably on account of his dress, that some person remarked to him, that he appeared to be endeavouring to walk in the footsteps of John Woolman,—a Friend with whom he had been intimately acquainted. After a pause, he said, "I am endeavouring to follow the footsteps of Christ."

William Boen, by attending to his Guide, and faithfully following Christ, his *new Master*, was brought to believe in his doctrine, in relation to gospel ministers: "Freely ye have received, freely give." He therefore did not approve of hireling ministry, or paying men for preaching. This testimony to a free gospel ministry, he carried so far, in order to keep a pure conscience towards his Divine Master, that on one occasion, after he had sold some wood to a person, who was called a clergyman,—he felt scrupulous about receiving money from him, which was obtained by preaching: as it would not be, in his apprehension, bearing a faithful testimony against hireling ministry. So he went to the man, and asked him whether he got his money by preaching. On being answered in the affirmative, William told him, he was not free to take his money in pay for the wood, as he did not approve of making money by preaching, contrary to the command of Christ.

Yet his mind was clothed with Christian charity towards his fellow creatures, who had not been brought to see and walk in the way which he apprehended to be required of him. William was not free to use any thing either in food or clothing, that he knew to be produced through the labour of slaves. On its being asked him, whether he thought so well of his friends that used the products of slavery, as he would do, if they did not use such articles; he replied, "*Obedience is all, with me.* I believe it is required of me, not to use these things: and if it has never been required of them, not to use these things, then they are as much in the way of their duty, in using them, as I am in the way of my duty, in not using them."

When William was drawing near the close of his long and exemplary life, his bodily powers failed through weakness, and the decay of nature; but his mind was preserved clear and tranquil. At this season, he was frequently visited by a friend, who, on one occasion, made some remarks respecting the calm and peaceful state of mind, which he appeared to enjoy, and inquired of him by what means he had attained to such a happy state. William, in accordance with his common expression of trying all things by the mind, gave this short and comprehensive answer: "By keeping the mind easy,—and resisting every thing that made it uneasy."

Soon after his death, the following obituary notice, appeared in one of the public papers:

"Died, near Mount Holly, on the 12th instant, in the ninetieth year of his age, William Boen (alias Heston), a coloured man."

Rare, indeed, are the instances that we meet with, in which we feel called upon to record the virtues of any of this afflicted race of people. The deceased, however, was one of those who had demonstrated the truth of that portion of scripture, that "of a truth God is no respecter of persons; but in every nation, they that fear him and work righteousness, are accepted with him."

He was concerned in early life, "to do justly, love mercy, and walk humbly with his God;" and by a close attention to the light of Christ within, and faithfully abiding under the operation of that blessed spirit of Divine grace in his soul, he was enabled, not only to bear many precious testimonies faithfully, to the end of his days, but also to bring forth those fruits of the spirit which redound to the glory of God, and the salvation of the soul. He was an exemplary member of the religious Society of Friends; and as he lived, so he died,—a rare pattern of a self-denying follower of Jesus Christ. He had no apparent disease,—either of body or mind; but, as he expressed himself a short time before his death, he felt nothing but weakness: which continued to increase,

until he gently breathed his last; and is, no doubt, entered into his heavenly Father's rest.

"Mark the perfect man, and behold the upright: for the end of that man is peace."

6th month, 1824.

Memorial of Mount Holly Monthly Meeting of Friends, concerning William Boen, a coloured man. Read in the Yearly Meeting of Friends, held in Philadelphia, 1829.

As the memory of those who have followed the leadings of that Teacher which leadeth into all truth, and enables its votaries to become, by example, preachers of righteousness, is precious, we feel engaged to give the following testimony concerning our deceased friend, William Boen, a coloured man.

He was born in the year 1735, in the neighbourhood of Rancocas. Being a slave from his birth, he had very little opportunity of acquiring useful learning; yet by his own industry and care, he succeeded in learning to read and write.

His mind became seriously impressed while very young, and he was induced in early life, to attend to the monitions of light and life in his own mind, being convinced from what he felt within him, of the existence of a Supreme Being; and also of the manner of his visiting the children of men, by the inward peace which he felt upon a faithful performance of what he thus apprehended to be his duty.

About the twenty-eighth year of his age, he contracted for his freedom; and having entered into marriage engagements with a woman in the neighbourhood, but not being, at that time, a member of our society, he was

John Woolman's house, near Mount Holly. From Barber and Howe, *Historical Collections of the State of New Jersey* (1844).

straitened in his mind how to accomplish it; as he was fully convinced of our testimony in that respect.

In this difficulty, he made known his situation to our friend, John Woolman, who, to relieve him, had a number of persons convened at a friend's house, where they were married after the manner of our society, and a certificate to that effect, furnished them by those present.

About this time he made application to become a member of our society; but way not opening in Friends' minds, he was not received, but encouraged to continue faithful; which we believe he did, from the account we have of nearly his whole life.

He was concerned above all things, to walk in the path of truth and righteousness; and according to his measure, to be faithful to every opening of duty, by which means he obtained the esteem of all who knew him.

As he thus continued steadfast to the light in his own mind, he was favoured to see the necessity of a daily cross to all the gratifications of self, and that the cause of truth cannot grow in us, while we are governed by a worldly spirit.

By yielding full obedience to that light, which it was his chiefest joy to follow, he became truly convinced of the necessity of maintaining the various testimonies which we, as a people, have been called upon to bear; and, in some respects, he had to bear a testimony against things in which many of his white brethren indulge, particularly in regard to slavery; refusing to wear, or use in any shape, articles which come through that corrupted channel. And, we believe, it was through dedication to the Lord, and an unreserved surrender of his will, to the Divine will, that he was brought to see these things in that light which deceiveth not. Thus, evincing by his

conversation and example, the truth of that scripture declaration, "All thy children shall be taught of the Lord, and great shall be the peace of thy children; in righteousness shalt thou be established."

It appears, not only from his own words, but also from his weighty example, that his great concern was to keep his mind easy, believing that right and wrong actions would result either in peace or pain within; hence, his great care was to "try all things by the mind," as he expressed it, or the light of Christ within; with which he was, no doubt, through faithfulness, in a remarkable manner favoured; esteeming it right to be obedient to every manifested duty, however in the cross, or insignificant to the carnal mind, these small duties might appear; and as he was found, like the servant in the parable, "faithful in the little," he was strengthened to rule over the carnal propensities of his nature, bringing his words and actions into the obedience of Christ. His humility was such, that although in low circumstances, he appeared to be content, and even refused to indulge himself in rich food or clothing, saying that "bread and water was good enough for him." In 1814, he was, on application, received into membership with us, and continued to the last, when able, a steady attender of our meetings, both for worship and discipline.

He enjoyed reasonable health and strength until about his eighty-seventh year, when his strength began to fail, but the faculties of his mind remained good until his end.

Some weeks previous to his death, he spoke of it with the utmost composure, and recounting his past trials and experiences said, "he had thought he was alone with regard to his testimony against slavery." But, as though

Friends Meeting House in Mount Holly, erected in 1775. *Courtesy of the Paul W. Schopp Collection.*

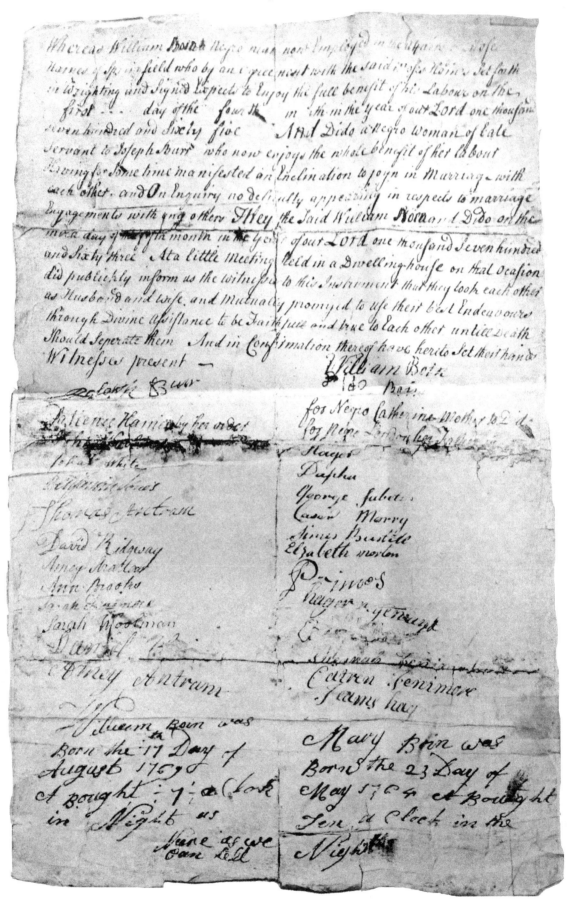

Quaker marriage certificate for John and Dido Boen, dated the third day of the fifth month, 1763. *Original certificate in the Quaker Collection, Haverford College.*

he had fresh evidences thereof, said, "he believed it would grow and increase among Friends." He appeared perfectly resigned to death, having no will therein; and as he expressed himself, "that some died hard and others easy, but for himself, he had no wish for either, being fully resigned to the Divine will in all things."

To a friend present, the day previous to his death, he stated "that he felt himself going very fast; but that he had no wish to stay." His weakness increasing, and having no desire to take any nourishment, he was asked if he was sick, or felt any pain; to which he answered, "that he felt neither pain nor sickness, but weakness, and a total disrelish for every thing of this world." His weakness continued to increase until he passed quietly away, on the night of the 12th of the 6th month, 1824, in the ninetieth year of his age; and we doubt not, he has entered into his heavenly Father's rest.

Read in, and approved by, Mount Holly Monthly Meeting of Friends, held 11th month 6th, 1828.

Amos Bullock, Clerk.

Read in, and approved by, Burlington Quarterly Meeting of Friends, held at Chesterfield, on the 25th of the 11th month, 1828, and directed to be forwarded to the Yearly Meeting.

Andrew C. Ridgway, Clerk.

Endnotes

Elizabeth M. Birch is a student at Stockton University and is pursuing a career in English Education.

Paul W. Schopp is the Assistant Director of the South Jersey Culture & History Center.

1   Amelia Mott Gummere, "Biographical Introduction," *The Journal and Essays of John Woolman, Rancocas Edition* (New York: The MacMillan Company, 1922), 83.
2   Donna McDaniel and Vanessa Julye, *Fit for Freedom, Not for Friendship: Quakers, African Americans, and the Myth of Racial Justice* (Philadelphia: Quaker Press, 2009), 188.

South Lakewood Sand Pit. Born in Sweden on September 1, 1860, Charles E. Peterson Sr. emigrated to the United States in 1872 and soon apprenticed in a Toms River cabinet shop. Armed with an entrepreneurial spirit, Peterson left cabinetry and became a collier, opened a sawmill, and sold real estate over time. In 1901, Charles began a sand mining operation at Mounts Crossing in South Lakewood, a.k.a. Whitesville, Ocean County, New Jersey. The mined sand proved ideal for use in the mixing of concrete. Peterson never formally incorporated the mining operation. He offered employment to from 12 to 20 men working in the sand pits. The men extracted the sand dry using a mechanical digger and conveyor. As seen in this circa 1912 view, a small industrial saddle-tank steam locomotive moved dump cars full of sand from the pits to storage facilities for transshipment on freight cars of the Central Railroad of New Jersey to fulfill customer orders. Workmen relocated the railroad tracks within the pits as needed to best accommodate the mining operations. Peterson maintained ownership of the sand-mining business until 1926, when, presumably, he sold out to the already extant Lakewood Sand Company, a firm that Somerville residents L. P. Gaston, Thomas Richards, and E. L. Richards formed in the early part of the twentieth century. A 1926 newspaper article describes the operation as "the largest single sand and gravel pits in the eastern states. . . ." The article continues by stating, "Hundreds of tons of valuable sand and gravel, which are used for paving road making and building purposes are excavated daily." Mr. Peterson pursued other businesses and lived to be 105, dying in 1966.

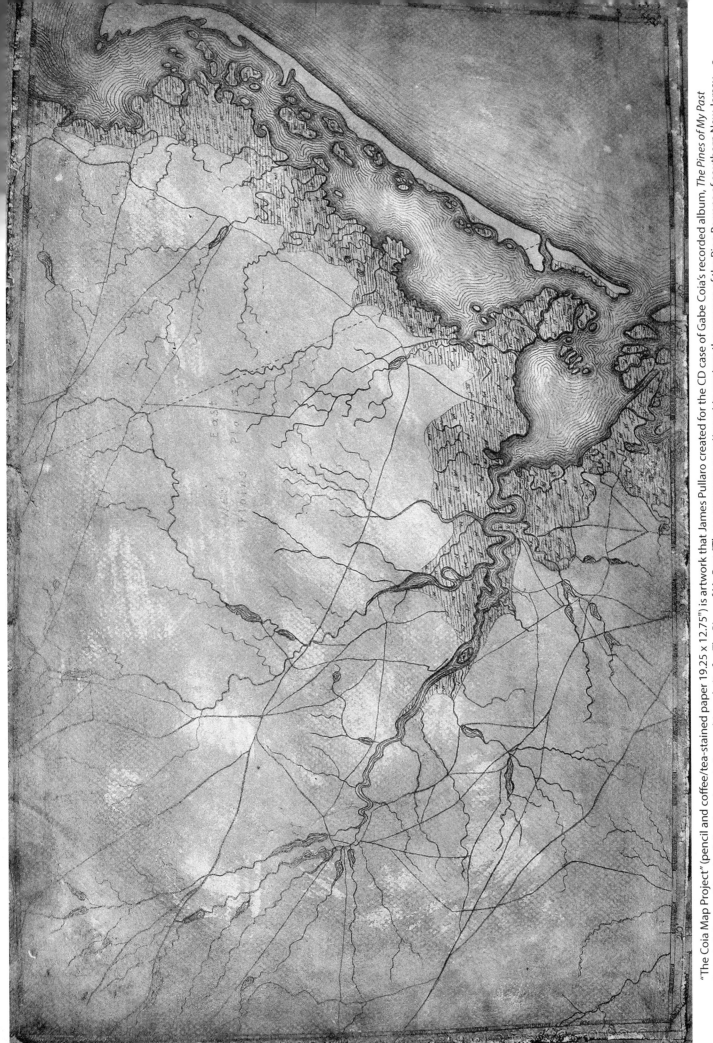

"The Coia Map Project" (pencil and coffee/tea-stained paper 19.25 x 12.75") is artwork that James Pullaro created for the CD case of Gabe Coia's recorded album, *The Pines of My Past* (2016). Gabe provides the following description on his website for *The Pines of My Past*: "These songs are my attempt to capture the essence of the Pine Barrens of southern New Jersey—a wilderness of haunting beauty where the distant past is ever-present."

The Coia Map Project

Artwork by James Pullaro, text by Paul W. Schopp

MAP PUBLISHING

The need for cartography—surveying and drawing maps—extends back at least 14,000 years as shown by the recent discovery of a stone tablet in a Spanish cave incised with representations of physical landscape features. Over the centuries, maps have served a wide variety of purposes, ranging from providing directions for reaching distant settlements or depicting geological deposits to defining property boundaries or navigating waterways. The emergence of GIS (Geographical Information System) software and its attendant datasets and layers over the past 40-plus years has broadened mapping purposes to manifold uses. Whether health officials employ GIS to track a pandemic or law enforcement officials study digital maps to identify crime hotspots, these powerful programs have leapfrogged the science of cartography into the twenty-first century and beyond.

Despite the modernity of current-day mapping techniques, many people remain fascinated with old or antique maps, the information they impart, and the methodologies employed to print them. Most early maps are strictly one-of-a-kind manuscript maps, but beginning in medieval times, printers used engraved wood blocks to produce published maps based on an original drawing. Engraved copper plates soon eclipsed the wood blocks. In both methods, the engraver cut or incised the design in reverse to provide a positive impression. When installed on the press and ready for use, ink would flow into the engraved lines of the wood or copper printing surface. When pressed against the paper, the ink formed raised lines in what is known as intaglio printing. Colorists, often female, added tinting to each printed map using watercolor washes.

In the late eighteenth century, a German actor and playwright named Alois Senefelder, reflecting on the old axiom, "oil and water do not mix," invented lithography as an inexpensive way of printing playbills. As its name suggests, the original printing "plate" was a block of smooth limestone. An artist would draw the design in reverse on the stone using a crayon containing oil, fat or wax. A wash of *gum Arabic* and acid solution across the stone would etch the entire surface except the areas featuring the grease-based design. The printer would install the stone in the press and moisten the surface, which prevented the oil-based ink from adhering to the stone except on the design. Again, colorists added tinting to these maps until the invention of chromolithography in the late nineteenth century diminished the use of hand coloring, although this labor-intensive handwork continued into the twentieth century. Lithography revolutionized printing, and subsequent technological advances, including the use of etched metal plates, made lithography the primary printing process during much of the nineteenth and twentieth centuries, although the relatively recent digital revolution has provided other printing methods in this modern age.

MAPPING OF NEW JERSEY

Pondering westward voyages from the European continent prior to 1492 always provides opportunities today for lively discussions, but it was Christopher Columbus's famous expedition of discovery that captured the imagination of royalty and the commoner in the nations of Europe. Cartographers worked quickly to offer visual representations of new lands—*terra incognita*—to those hungering for more knowledge. The landmass of present-day New Jersey appears as an unformed blob on early maps, particularly for those depicting large swaths of territory. As the cartographers of Europe obtained information from mariners and copied details of maps from each other, New Jersey gradually acquired its more familiar shape as mapmakers worked with more accuracy. Dutch cartographers and printers led the world in publishing maps of the New World, and the Mid-Atlantic portion of America in particular, to show its colony of New Netherland and its capital, New Amsterdam. Since New Netherland included all the lands down to the Delaware Bay, New Jersey appeared with regularity and in a more refined form as part of these Dutch maps.

When the English captured New Netherland in 1664 without firing a shot, the former Hollander colony became the property of Charles II as king of Great Britain. London cartographer John Sellers was the first mapmaker to publish a stand-alone *Mapp of New Jarsey*. This was one of the first maps to label the colony as New Jersey and its neighbor as New York. Other published maps followed during the seventeenth and eighteenth centuries, with Charing Cross mapmaker John Faden's 1777 map, *The Province of New Jersey Divided into East and West, Commonly Called The Jerseys*, being among the most well-known of New Jersey maps from the colonial period. Faden issued a greatly revised edition of this map in December 1778. Despite the fine appearance of the Faden map, it contains considerable geographical errors.

In 1799, the state legislature approved an act to incorporate a company to create "... an accurate map of the State of New-Jersey," with the stipulation that the map must be in print by 1803, but nothing came of this effort. William Watson of Gloucester County published a map in 1812 filled with errors and assumptions. New Jersey legislators made another attempt to obtain an accurate map of the state in 1822 when the lawmakers approved a loan of $1000 to Trenton surveyor and cartographer Thomas Gordon, provided he repaid the money within two years without interest. Gordon set out to conduct original surveys and collect surveys performed by others to assemble his map. When completed, Gordon turned over his manuscript map to Henry S. Tanner, a cartographer, engraver and publisher of some note in Philadelphia. Tanner engraved Thomas Gordon's map on three copper plates for printing the finished map. Writing about Gordon's map in his 1973 work, *The Mapping of New Jersey: The Men and the Art*, author John P. Snyder notes:

> This time the result was monumental. In 1828, Gordon produced a high quality *A Map of the State of New Jersey* at a scale of 3 miles/inch. H. S. Tanner was the engraver. All townships are shown with considerable care. The emerging turnpike system is given distinctive marking. With half-inch-wide traces, counties are bordered in red, green, orange, or yellow. Township borders received narrow strips of color, different for adjacent townships.... New Jersey mapping had achieved a new high.

As the time to release his map drew near, Thomas Gordon placed the following notice in the *Emporium and True American*, published in Trenton:

Map of New-Jersey,

With part of the adjoining States, compiled, under the patronage of said state, by Thomas Gordon, will be published on the 15th inst. by the author, Trenton, and H S. Tanner, Philadelphia. It is projected on a scale of 3 miles to 1 inch, and engraved on three large sheets, presenting such a view of all the counties, townships, towns, churches, roads, mountains, streams, mills, canals, &c. as cannot fail to give general satisfaction.

April 8, 1828.   58-3t.

Gordon released a revised edition of his map in 1833 and a third edition in 1850. Robert E. Hornor released the fourth and final edition of Gordon's map. The quality of this publication served as the most authoritative map of New Jersey for 30 years, when cartographers began using the geodetic surveying method to produce published maps featuring an even higher degree of accuracy.

JAMES PULLARO'S ARTWORK

The artwork presented on page 94 stems from the mind and incredible abilities of accomplished artist James Pullaro, whose love and passion for the New Jersey Pine Barrens has had a huge impact on his life and his art. Based on Thomas Gordon's original 1828 map of the state, James sought to illustrate the Mullica River watershed. This work is not a mere reproduction of what Gordon had prepared. Rather, James embarked on a process to achieve his finished artwork. Here is that process in his own words:

> I call it "The Coia Map Project" as it had been originally created for Gabe Coia's recording album entitled *The Pines of My Past*. Starting with a new piece of paper, my first objective was to distress it to create the illusion that it was centuries old. To accomplish that, I took sandpaper to it, scraped the edges, and generally handled it roughly. I used coffee and tea to stain it to achieve that aged tone. The original artwork measures 19.25" x 12.75". The medium is graphite, ink, tea, and coffee. The map features are modeled after the Thomas Gordon 1828 map. The General tonal effects are modeled mostly after the 1812 Watson map. I somewhat combined time periods so that more dams could be represented. I wanted to be more inclusive on one map and show the many locations of manufacture by waterpower. I also wanted the map to be somewhat timeless, helping to lend the mysterious nature of an old treasure map in the best tradition of *"Aarrghh ... thar be draguns here!"*

It is fair to say that James more than accomplished what he set out to do with his artwork!

Call for Articles

The South Jersey Culture & History Center at Stockton University publishes twice-yearly issues of *SoJourn*. We actively seek community members, avocational historians, and scholars to contribute essays on topics related to South Jersey. Illustrations to accompany these articles will be a plus. Articles should be written for laypersons who are interested and curious about South Jersey topics, but do not necessarily have expertise in the areas covered. Potential authors should check SJCHC's website for a link to a simplified style sheet guide for article preparation—www.stockton.edu/sjchc/—or just follow the style in this issue. Journal editors will be happy to guide any would-be authors. In certain instances, Stockton editing interns may be assigned to help research topics and/or assist authors with writing.

Sample topics might include:
Biographical sketches of important but forgotten local people; the development or succession of a community's roads, bridges or buildings; local transportation (focused by mode, area or era) and what changes it wrought in the served communities; history of community businesses and industries (wineries, garment factories, agriculture, boat building, clamming, etc.); old school houses, old hotels, or meeting halls; narrative descriptions of local geographical features; essays concerned with folklore, music, arts; and reviews of new local interest publications. Photo essays and old photograph and postcard reproductions are welcome with applicable captions. In short, if a South Jersey topic interests you, it will likely interest *SoJourn*'s readers.

Parameters for submissions:
• Submissions must pertain to topics bounded within the 8 southernmost counties of New Jersey (Burlington & Ocean Counties and south)
• Manuscripts should be approximately 3,000 – 4,000 words long (5 to 7 pages of single-spaced text and 9 to 12 pages including images)
• Manuscripts should conform to the *SoJourn* style sheet, available here: https://blogs.stockton.edu/sjchc/sojourn-style-sheet/
• Manuscripts, if at all possible, should be submitted in digital format (Word- or pdf-formatted documents preferred)
• Images should be submitted as high-resolution tiff- or jpeg-formatted files (editors can assist with digital conversion of photos if necessary)
• Complete and appropriate citations printed as endnotes should be employed (see style sheet)
• Original submissions only. Copyright licenses for all images must be obtained by the author or should be copyright-free figures and/or figures in the public domain
• If essays are accepted, authors should submit a short 50 to 100 word autobiographical statement
• Articles need to be more than just a chronology of the given topic. The author should be able to properly contextualize the subject by answering such questions as: a) why is this important?; b) what is the impact on the local or regional history? and c) how does it compare to similar events/personages/changes/processes in other localities?

Call for submissions:
Submissions for fall issues are due before September 1; for spring issues, January 15. Send inquiries or submissions to Thomas.Kinsella@stockton.edu or Paul.Schopp@stockton.edu.

Notes and Queries: Finally, we invite readers to submit brief notes of interest or queries about topics of South Jersey history to either of the two editors named immediately above.

CPSIA information can be obtained
at www.ICGtesting.com
Printed in the USA
BVOW05s0252180717

489548BV00008B/15/P

9 780997 669985